TO: ANNE
CAR
JONAH, AND OWEN

LOVE,
Dad Dad Mom T.

❧ The Move of a Lifetime ❧
Moving Frank Lake Covenant Church

KATHY A. WECKWERTH

The History of
Frank Lake Covenant
&

The Journey to Become
The Church in the Grove

❧ The Move of a Lifetime ❦
Moving Frank Lake Covenant Church

© 2017 Kathy A. Weckwerth.
All rights reserved.

No portion of this book may be reproduced, stored in a retrieval system,
or transmitted in any form or by any means - electronic, mechanical, photocopy,
recording, or any other - except for brief quotation in printed reviews,
without the prior permission of the publisher.

Published by Kathy Weckwerth, PO Box 73, Benson, MN 56215

Cover Design: Peter Grossman
Editors: Marlene Giese & Susan C. Snow
Interior Layout: Susan C. Snow
Photography: Alexis Iskierka & Kathy A. Weckwerth
Back Cover Photo: Kathy A. Weckwerth

Some Photos: Courtesy of Covenant Archives and Historical Library,
North Park University, Chicago.

Other Photos: Grateful acknowledgement is given to families and friends
for sharing their personal historical photographs

All Scripture references are taken from the following sources:

The New International Version of the Bible (NIV)
© 1984 by the International Bible Society.
Used by permission of Zondervan Bible Publishers.

The Message Copyright © by Eugene H. Peterson 1993, 1994, 1995,
1996, 2000, 2001, 2002. Used by permission of NavPress Publishing
Group.

Visit the author's website: www.KathyWeckwerth.com
Visit the author's ministry website: www.BestLifeMinistries.com

ISBN: 978-0-692-92007-7

❧

*T*his book is dedicated to all the congregants and pastors

Who made up the life of Frank Lake Covenant Church,

To Farmer Dean who gave up his grove,

To my friends and neighbors who supported us,

And to God, the ultimate

Redeemer, Restorer,

Rebuilder **and** ***Renovator* ...**

*T*hank you from the bottom of my heart.

Let the journey continue.

❧ The author at *Frank Lake Covenant* now *Church in the Grove* ❧

❧ The Move of a Lifetime ❧
Moving Frank Lake Covenant Church

Introduction	1
Planting The Dream	5
The Church Burns	11
The Church Building	17
The Pastors	25
The People	47
The Search	71
Buying the Church	79
The Foundation	87
The Route	93
The Cleaning	97
The Goodbye Service	101
The Preparation	109
The Neighbors	119
The Move	123
The Steeple	137
The Restoration	141
The Visitors	151
The Journey Continues	163

❧ The Introduction ❧

For the Lord is good and His love endures forever;
His faithfulness continues through all generations.
Psalm 100:5

In a day and age where church was the revolving force which made families stronger, neighbors connected, and lives fervently keeping God at the center of life itself, a small, plain white building was erected in the middle of farm country, a stone's throw from the lake that gave it its namesake. Frank Lake Covenant Church stood tall and proud for 112 years outside of rural Murdock, Minnesota.

That is, until it took a journey through country roads, over hills, across bridges, traveling twenty-six miles to make its way to our little grove south of Benson, Minnesota, thus becoming the Church in the Grove, and an essential part of my story.

Across the years, the origin of the church's story is a testament to those who have gone before, a tribute to those whose lives were woven into the tapestry of the beautiful history that makes up the story of Frank Lake Covenant Church.

This is the journey of how the life of one little church came to be moved after a 32-year respite. Its congregation was known for its amazingly beautiful musical abilities and power-filled preaching for 80 years. The move allowed it to once again regain its purpose and open its doors to those who are seeking a Savior.

In the deepest places of my heart and soul, in the inner crevices of my mind where hopes and dreams exist, I could never believe that someday my husband and I would own this exquisite building. Nor would I believe that it would sit in our grove and serve its purpose of honoring God. But dreams often do come to reality for those who look up at the sky and pray for miracles.

I embrace each and every day that I look out the family room window and see the roof and steeple towering above the trees, silhouetted against a bright blue sky, reflecting rays of light and hope with each moment it stands erect before God's heaven.

Within these pages, I make my best effort to walk you through the life of one little country church. But this story doesn't limit itself to the lovely purple and yellow stained glass windows, or the vaulted tin ceiling, or the beautiful light fixtures.

No, it takes you through the moments that are lived within the very walls and windows that make up the little church. Because life doesn't merely exist outside the structures of our bodies and buildings, but instead is made up of days and nights of living, breathing, worshiping, praying, and the relationships we hold dear with one another and our Heavenly Father.

Let these moments of memories, these glimpses and snapshots into lives of those who went before us to create a purpose and a plan for one small church, rise up and reach us in the deepest places of our inner being. Know that God, in His infinite wisdom, wasn't quite finished with the purpose of Frank Lake Covenant. No, He had a plan.

He Himself would blow fresh God-wind into a quiet, restful, spot in the middle of the countryside, where time had stood still and memories were silently waiting to resume in the hearts and minds of friends, neighbors, and family.

This church means so much to my husband, Dean, and to me. It has not just clearly represented God at work in our everyday lives, but it has drawn us closer to new friends and a history that had become dusty on the bookcase shelves of this old world.

This little building has become a representation of how God works in the quiet times when everyone else has forgotten us. It has become a place where we continue the vision that was cast in 1877, directly from the hearts of men who saw a need to deliver the good news of salvation.

Dean and I happily received the baton that God thrust into our hands back in the spring of 2012 to continue to use it for a purpose ... *God's purpose*.

Each day, when we walk through the double doors of this sweet church, we commit to God our thoughts, our deeds, our hopes, our desires, as we present His Word, and we press into the challenge that has been placed before us.

It's in Your hands we commit this building. May its purpose serve You continually as it has done ... from generation to generation.

Welcome, God
Welcome to the Past
Welcome to the Present
Welcome to the Future

❧ Frank Lake Covenant Church Congregation ❧
circa 1917

Frank Lake Covenant Church Congregation
Rev. Albin Nelson
circa 1939

❧ Planting The Dream ❧

*I will instruct you and teach you in the way you should go;
I will counsel you with my eye upon you.*
Psalm 32:8

In the late 1870s, a group of Swedish pioneers made their way to settle in rural Murdock, Minnesota. When they saw the beauty of a small lake named Frank Lake, they began to buy their fields and build their homes and a community erupted out of the deep rich earth, as farmers planted seeds of dreams.

A pioneer named C. M. Youngquist felt a deep, strong calling to deliver the gospel of Jesus Christ to the small rural area. As he visited Murdock, Minnesota, the Spirit of God delivered a plan and Youngquist began to hold meetings in various homes and then at the little country schoolhouse.

Youngquist visited the community as a traveling pastor, preaching the Word of God and salvation through Jesus Christ as Savior. Records from the late 1800's report that there was a genuine spirit of revival in the hearts of those early pioneers and distance meant nothing to them as the Holy Spirit was working in their hearts. Many of them came as far as 75 miles to attend revival meetings. Church services were held in various homes and in the District 40 schoolhouse whenever visiting pastors such as Youngquist came through the area.

On January 12, 1884, one cold Minnesota evening, a committee met to create and organize a church congregation. They worked out a constitution for the purpose of organizing the "Swedish Missions Kyrkan's" church as a permanent congregation.

This committee brought a report to a subsequent meeting held on June 2, 1884. With 55 members by June of that year, and since the church was to be positioned across the road from Frank Lake, the group settled on the name "Swedish Evangelical Mission Church of Frank Lake, Murdock, Minnesota."

Frank Lake was thought to have received its name from one of two early settlers, Frank Harstad or Frank Vast, who was thought to have been the earliest settler to the area.

❧ Frank Lake, Murdock, Minnesota ❧

That first board consisted of the following: Deacons: Olaus Olson Berg, Andrew Johnson, Axel Anderson; secretary: Charles Johnson; trustees: L. P. Larson, Edwin Danielson, and August Johnson. Olaus Olson Berg served as the first chairman of the church board and on May 25, 1885, they voted and called A. Sundberg as their first pastor. The congregation continued to meet in private homes and the nearby schoolhouse.

Church records written on September 4, 1887, indicate that the settlers firmly planted their feet on a path that would lead them to building a small church. The site would be in Kerkhoven Township, Swift County, across from Frank Lake. A man named Charles Ellson (known as Snickare Charlie) built the church.

This document also states that the following men agreed to be responsible for the sacred and healthy development of the church at large: Charles Johnson, Olaus Olson Berg, John Mellgren, and Charles Dahl.

With excitement and sheer joy, the board continued to move forward with their plan. It was the middle of spring on a warm sunny May day, the 29th of the month, in the year 1888, when John Wass sold a parcel of land to The Swedish Evangelical Mission Society of Frank Lake, Swift County, Minnesota. And for such a time as this, a group of Swedish immigrants living in the rural countryside near Murdock, Minnesota, planted their dream and it began to take root.

A dream had unfolded.

A purpose given.

The dedication service was held with the Rev. C. M. Youngquist, as speaker. Youngquist was there firsthand to see God's faithfulness in fulfilling the vision God had bestowed upon this young minister.

The happy Rev. C. M. Youngquist returned to where his dream seeds had been planted and he spoke to the congregation encouraging them at their dedication of the church building. As he looked out over the crowd, his heart was filled with a grateful attitude towards our great dream-providing God. A God who fills our hearts and minds with desires, and helps us succeed in reaching those goals.

 Rev. Charles Magnus Youngquist

The breezes of new life were blowing through the windows and rafters of the Swedish Evangelical Mission Church of Frank Lake, Murdock, MN.

Life in rural America was challenging with farmers relying on weather for good crops and working to keep farm equipment maintained and safe to use. Many physical illnesses and diseases could take young lives within days, so families desperately tried to keep their children safe and healthy.

But for most of the neighbors who lived within close proximity to the church, their lives continued to be filled with the Sunday morning and evening services, along with special meetings at the little church. Day-to-day life focused around farm, family and faith. The church was the center of their social life and their faith was the soul compass for how they lived their lives. Hand-in-hand it all went and days ticked on as life in rural Murdock continued with their eyes upon God.

❧ Original Sign from the Site ☙
Located Above the Entrance at Church in the Grove

Original Constitution

Translation

Forsamlingens namn:
Svenska Missions Forsmling
Frank Lake Assembly Name:
Swedish Missions Assembly Frank Lake

Antal medlemmar da: 10
Numbers of members men: 10

Antal medlemmar ma: 40
Number of members women: 40

Kyrka byggd nar: 1889
Church built when: 1889

Ny kyrka byggd nar: 1889
New church built when: 1899

Sondagsskola begynt nar: 1883
Begun when: 1883

Antal barn: 15
Number of children: 15

Antal larare: 1
Number of teachers: 1

Namn pa forsamlingens forsta styrelse:
Name the assembly first board:
O. O. Berg, Ard Axel Anderson, Sec. Charles Johnson, Andrew Johnson and August Johnson, Trustee L. P. Larson, Edwin Danielson and O.O. Berg Deacon.

Namn pa de predikanter som betjanat fornanlingen:
Name of the ministers who served the former trend: C.M. Youngquist, H. Sunberg, Nils Frykman, Theo Steinert, A.W. Carlson

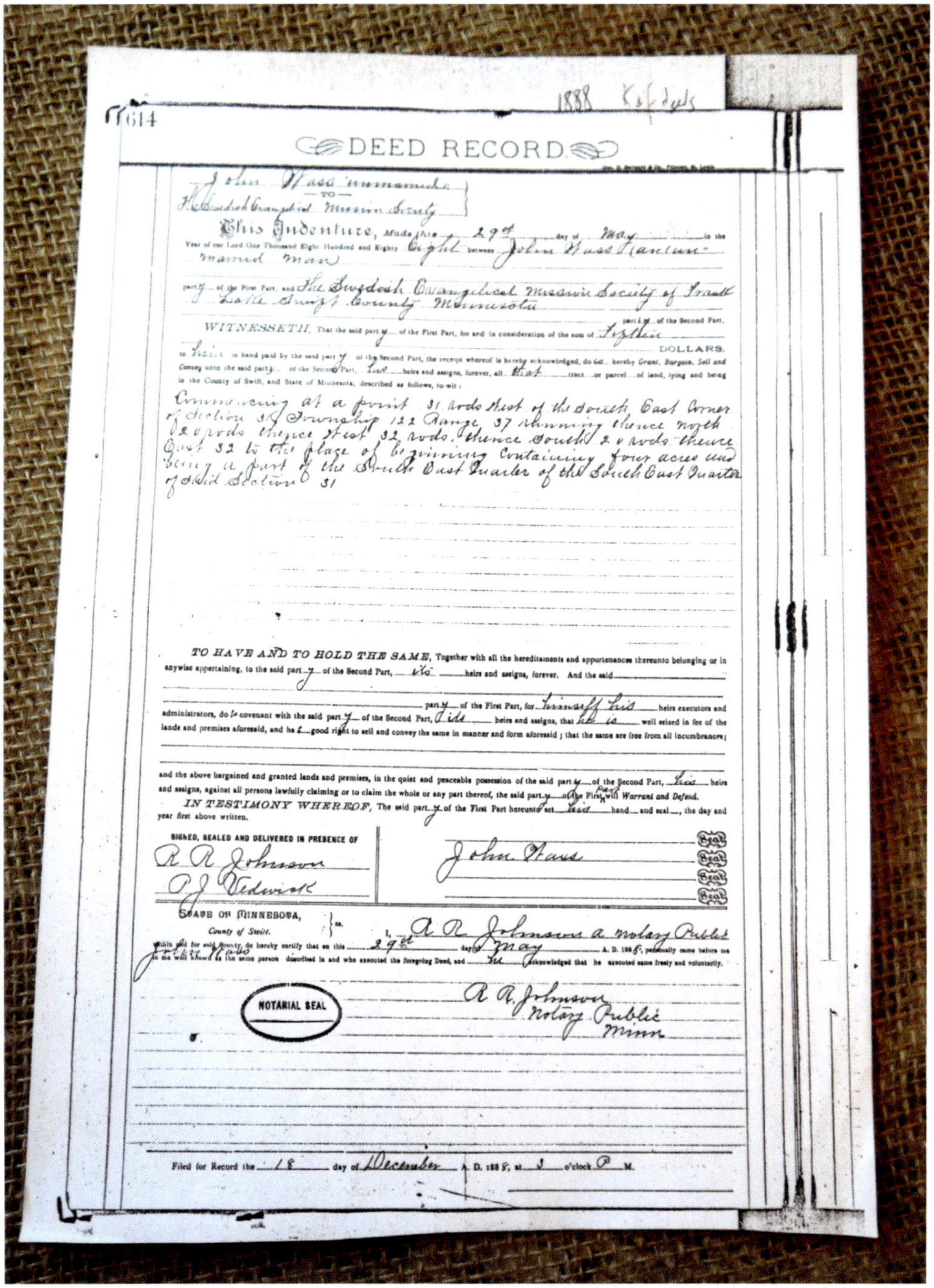
614

1888 K of deeds

DEED RECORD

John Wass unmarried
— TO —
The Swedish Evangelical Mission Society

This Indenture, Made this 29th day of May in the Year of our Lord One Thousand Eight Hundred and Eighty Eight between John Wass unmarried man party of the First Part, and The Swedish Evangelical Mission Society of Frank Lake Swift County Minnesota party of the Second Part,

WITNESSETH, That the said party of the First Part, for and in consideration of the sum of Fifteen DOLLARS, to him in hand paid by the said party of the Second Part, the receipt whereof is hereby acknowledged, does hereby Grant, Bargain, Sell and Convey unto the said party of the Second Part, his heirs and assigns, forever, all that tract or parcel of land, lying and being in the County of Swift, and State of Minnesota, described as follows, to-wit:

Commencing at a point 31 rods West of the South East Corner of Section 31 Township 122 Range 37 running thence north 20 rods thence West 32 rods thence South 20 rods thence East 32 to the place of beginning Containing four acres and being a part of the South East Quarter of the South East Quarter of said Section 31

TO HAVE AND TO HOLD THE SAME, Together with all the hereditaments and appurtenances thereunto belonging or in anywise appertaining, to the said party of the Second Part, his heirs and assigns, forever. And the said party of the First Part, for himself his heirs executors and administrators, does covenant with the said party of the Second Part, his heirs and assigns, that he is well seized in fee of the lands and premises aforesaid, and has good right to sell and convey the same in manner and form aforesaid; that the same are free from all incumbrances;

and the above bargained and granted lands and premises, in the quiet and peaceable possession of the said party of the Second Part, his heirs and assigns, against all persons lawfully claiming or to claim the whole or any part thereof, the said party of the First Part will Warrant and Defend.

IN TESTIMONY WHEREOF, The said party of the First Part hereunto set his hand and seal, the day and year first above written.

SIGNED, SEALED AND DELIVERED IN PRESENCE OF
A. R. Johnson
P. J. Vedwick

John Wass (Seal)

STATE OF MINNESOTA, County of Swift. } ss.
I, A. R. Johnson a Notary Public within and for said County, do hereby certify that on this 29th day of May A. D. 1888, personally came before me John Wass to me well known as the same person described in and who executed the foregoing Deed, and he acknowledged that he executed same freely and voluntarily.

NOTARIAL SEAL

A. R. Johnson
Notary Public
Minn

Filed for Record the 18 day of December A. D. 1888, at 3 o'clock P. M.

Original Land Deed

The Swedish Evangelical Mission Society of Frank Lake

Swift County
Minnesota

Purchased Land
from John Wass

Price $15

May 29, 1888

Map Featuring Frank Lake

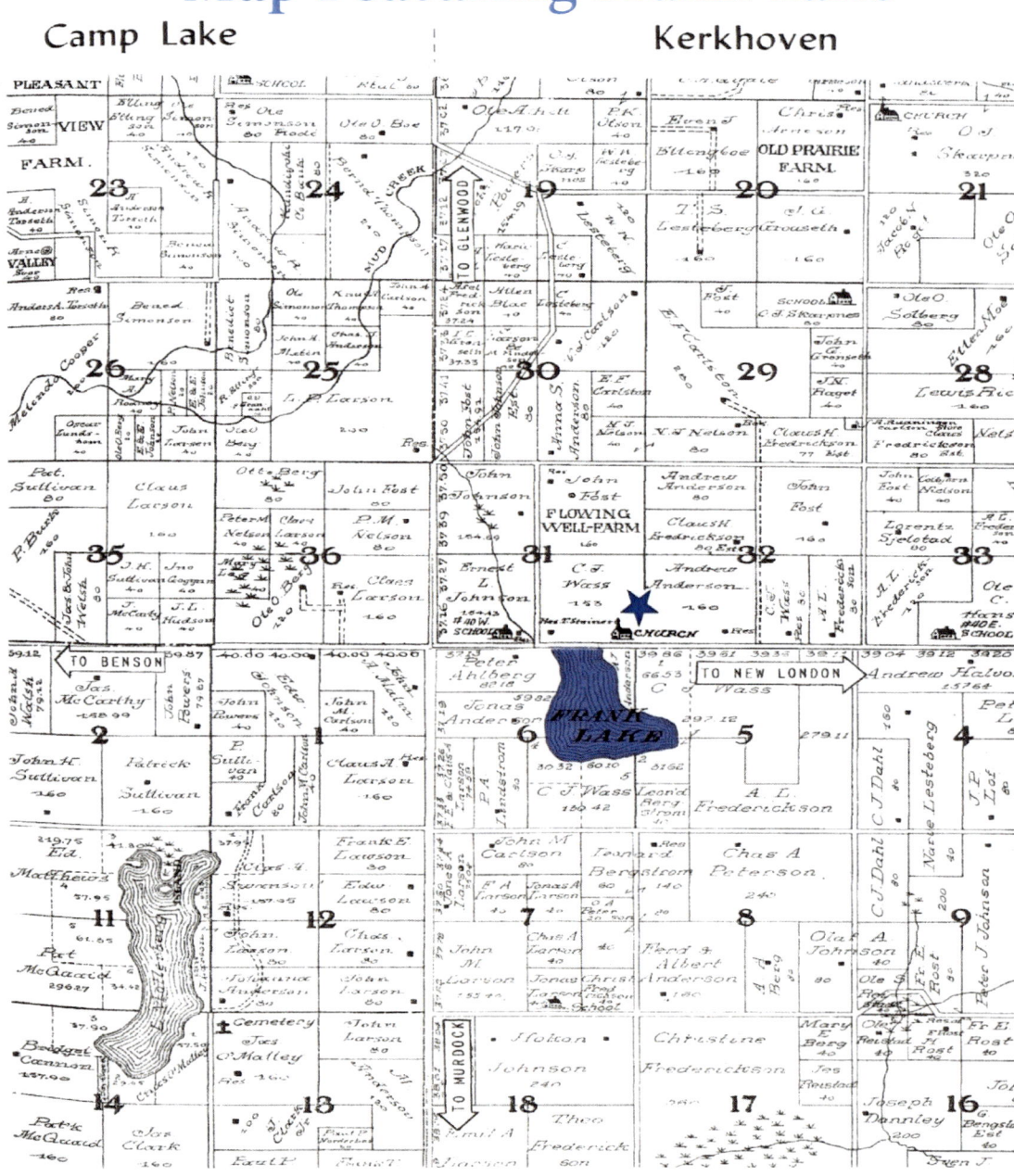

~ The Church Burns ~

*Now may the God of hope fill you with all joy and peace in believing,
that ye may abound in hope, through the power of the Holy Ghost.*
Romans 15:13

In January of 1890, the church called Reverend Nils Frykman to serve Frank Lake Covenant along with four other churches in what was known as "The Salem Circuit." This included Salem Covenant, Lake Florida, Lundby and West Lake.

~ Rev. Nils Frykman ~

The church was growing, the flock flourishing, and the Reverend Nils was adding life, creativity and music to the services, as he wrote many hymns while traveling country roads from church to church.

But sometimes life's journey will take a turn and a twist, and not all roads are smooth and easily accessible. As life often sends challenges, the congregation was hit with a strong shaking of their faith when a horrific storm in June of 1900 settled into the area. With the beloved church being a mainstay of focus for the congregation, imagine the shock, horror and fear that settled into the hearts and minds of those dear parishioners.

As farmers quickly hurried their animals into barns for shelter, people watched heavy rains and harsh winds strike. But no one suspected that lightening would be the culprit of destruction for the recently-built church.

One of the parishioners, Vernie Larson Swenson was a young girl of eight at the time. She later wrote in a personal journal:

What could have caused the fire that would destroy our church, that I no longer know — if ever we did know. Perhaps it could have been struck by lightning during one of the spectacular electrical storms of that locality — though I remember no rain. But suddenly there came someone galloping into our farmyard on horseback—not at all a usual mode of travel, shouting "Kyrkan brinner! Kyrkan brinner (which meant the church is burning). Tell the men! Bring buckets!

"Come quickly!" and like Paul Revere, he hastened on to Grandpa's, to Uncle Edwin's. Our men-folk dashed off; Mama and Ella and Ethel ran about with hapless aimlessness; weeping, praying, wringing at their aprons. And I was weeping; too—it seemed the end of the world that our church should be on fire. Frantically the men formed rope and bucket brigades to relay water up from the lake; it was at best a futile effort at such distance; the building was razed quite to the ground.

All was destroyed except their beautiful organ, which a parishioner described in journals as *"a husky young man named Ernest Johnson pulled through a window to rescue."*

There are times when humans wonder and question God. Why would He put a dream in the soul if the dream so quickly comes to an end? Why would the difficult-to-raise monies blow away with the stormy winds? Did the group perhaps not hear the voice of God at all?

Vernie remembered being an eight-year-old child when the church burned in this journal entry:

Weeks later, during the noon recess from school, we children wandered the half-mile or so past the lake to poke about the ruined foundations where the church had stood. And there I picked up a fused lump of glass. It was a pale blue; it would have been a part of one of the window panes.

❧ Vernie Larson Swenson with Her Cats ☙

Without a church building after the June 1900 lightning strike, the church members continued meeting in homes as they had done when they first began. Hearts were discouraged, but they knew that the future held promise.

After much deliberation, the church leaders, as well as anxious family members, decided to rebuild the church and raised $2,000 to cover the costs. At the same time, they purchased the pews and the pulpit that are still being utilized at the Church in the Grove today.

Church members and neighbors used horses to haul field stone from nearby fields to use as the foundation. They also loaded wagons full of lumber to build the church and horses brought the loads to the site.

With feet firmly planted in the gospel, and their faith strengthened in their continued meetings, the families bonded together over the tragedy and determination grew more than it had before. It made them stronger.

The storm had destroyed their building and cast down their spirits. But when the light of day broke, they rescued something tangible ... something real.

Several months later, the new building was erected and worship continued on as before at the Evangelical Mission Church of Frank Lake, Murdock, Minnesota.

*T*hey rescued the part of their church that could not be destroyed ...

*T*heir faith in a God who loved them.

❧ Frykmans' Pennock Parsonage ❦

❧ Original Swedish Choir 1898 ☙

Back: Alfred Berg, Claude Larson, Fred Anderson, Ernest Johnson, Thure Larson, Walfred Johnson

Front: Alice Anderson Magnuson, Ellen Larson, Otto Berg, Ella Larson, Mary Edelia Fost

❧ Frank Lake's Original Organ ✍
Currently at the Swift County
Historical Museum
Benson, Minnesota

❧ Ernest Johnson ✍
Saved the Organ
from the
Flames in 1900

❧ The Choir Girls ✍
Dianne Larson, Janice Olson, Jennifer Larson, Charlotte Forsell

❧ The Church Building ❧

*Not giving up meeting together, as some are in the habit of doing,
but encouraging one another—
and all the more as you see the day approaching.
Hebrews 10:25*

❧ Frank Lake Church ❧
circa 1909

Historians report that the Covenant churches from the early 1900s had very simple designs for their buildings. Whether it was plain arched windows, solid oak front doors, basic white paint, or steeples with a single bell, the exteriors of this denomination's buildings were very similar.

Unlike its neighboring churches, Frank Lake Covenant stood peacefully with a plain clad exterior and a lovely simplistic interior design. The interiors of the Covenant church buildings had no wooden crosses, no huge pipe organs, no big decorative urns, no built-in podiums, and no kneeling pads included. No carved sculptures of cherubim and seraphim. No baby Jesus and Mother Mary. No altars were made.

Instead, the stage held two large chairs for the pastor and deacon to sit on, a simple piano, a basic organ, and one large oak pulpit from which the pastor preached. In many of the churches, displayed on the wall directly behind the pastor's pulpit, hung Warner Sallman's paintings entitled *Head of Christ* or *Christ at Heart's Door*. A painting would have replaced a large cross found in many other churches. Just simplistic walls and windows, pews and organ were housed, much as the tradition of minimalistic Covenanters.

Frank Lake Covenant's building was simplistic in design in comparison to many other country churches. The congregation decided on constructing a sanctuary and one additional room. Almost half the size of the large sanctuary, the spacious room was built on the right-hand side of the church.

A six-sided steeple was built to host a large bell that would sound throughout the countryside, while a small wind vane sat perched atop the steeple. A steep pitch was created on the roofline to help with heavy snow that could accumulate in Minnesota winters.

❧ Stained Glass Window ☙
circa 1900

The building was painted white and small round windows were inserted on the south and east sides. Large opaque windows were created with majestic hues of purple and gold art glass. Two heavy oak doors, painted white on the outside and left natural on the inside, made a warm welcoming entrance to the little building.

The building stood 40'x 36' with a roomy entryway made of beadboard and double doors that lead into the sanctuary. Centered along the north wall was a small stage built out of quarter sawn oak in the shape of a half moon.

In the center of the stage hung a simple copy of *Christ at Heart's Door* painting based on Revelation 3:20, "Behold, I stand at the door and knock ..." Created by artist Warner Sallman *(circa early 1940s)* it depicts Jesus knocking at a door and served the Frank Lake congregation for 75 years. The artwork continues to hang in place today at the Church in the Grove.

A large woodstove stood in the center of the church and served to heat the building. A big accordion door would be pulled across to separate the sanctuary and the side room so as to host the children's Sunday school classes.

Later on, the side room would hold a large electric stove and counter to serve refreshments at funerals and potluck meals. At the back of that same room, a plain white oak door with a lovely glass knob was installed to lead out the back of the church to the cemetery.

In the fall of 1900, the congregation purchased pews and a sturdy but plain oak pulpit that would house such preachers as Nils Frykman, Theodore Steinert, and A.W. Carlson.

In 1917, while Rev. Arvid Ostling served as pastor of Frank Lake Covenant Church, the piano was purchased and placed on the right side of the stage.

In 1924, during the leadership of Rev. S. E. Roslin, the church building received an almost complete renovation when the main auditorium was redecorated with pressed tin sheeting and the exterior of the building was given a fresh coat of white paint.

❧ Current Entrance ☙

In 1939, under the leadership of Pastor Albin E. Nelson, electricity was installed in both the church and the parsonage. Three large hanging light fixtures were displayed down the center of the sanctuary to add light and a hue of warmth. Two small sconces reflected soft light upon the altar, while two large circular light fixtures attached directly to the ceiling in the side room.

ꙮ Light Fixtures Installed 1939 ꙮ
The Art Glass Windows & Light Fixtures Remain Intact

With Rev. Eddie R. Stenlund beginning his pastoral role on October 21, 1945, the church redecorated the interior and installed an electric oil furnace, while shrubs were planted outside the building.

Many years later between 1960-1967, during his time of service to the church, carpenter/Rev. Edwin Johnson rallied a group of men to work with him in yet another renovation, this time a modernization of the sanctuary.

By the late 1970s, two large furnaces were placed in front of the back door that led out to the cemetery, and served until their removal in 2015.

❧ 1970's Furnaces ❧

Frank Lake Covenant Church, no matter if adorned in snowy winter whites or lavished in the backdrop of blue skies and puffy white clouds, always portrayed a simpler mindset.

It possessed a mindset where bricks and mortar couldn't define it.

It most certainly didn't portray a mindset where its large towering steeple cried out,

"I'm here. Look at me, look at me."

Frank Lake Covenant possessed a quieter, more peaceful appearance,
as if to somehow call to a neighboring soul and quietly whisper,

"I'm here. Look at Him, look at Him."

❧ Evangelical Covenant Pastors 1903 ❦

Standing: Sven A. Youngquist, Aaron Carlson, C. G. Peterson,
S. A. Matson, John Wenstrand, C. Wallbom
Sitting: Axel Mellander, Carl A. Bjork, **Nils Frykman**, David Nyvall

❧ The Pastors ☙

*Let us not become weary in doing good,
for at the proper time we will reap a harvest
if we do not give up.
Galatians 6:9*

I believe that in the life of every church, God has ordained the moments in time and space where certain people are called to that body of believers, to serve, to love, and to lead.

Within the pages of the history of Frank Lake Covenant, it was an interesting journey to locate and study each of the men who served behind the pulpit on Sunday mornings, Sunday nights, and Wednesday evenings.

In taking a closer look, I found that each of these men had many different gifts and talents needed for different moments on the timeline of the life of the church.

Frank Lake Covenant Church was blessed with many good pastors throughout the years. These men were faith-filled, gospel preaching, tenacious men of God. Many of them served as circuit pastors driving horse and buggy from one church to a neighboring church, Sunday after Sunday.

Churches could not separately afford pastors and utilized the same pastor to serve their churches. Many churches, such as Frank Lake Covenant, shared pastors throughout a span of eighty years.

In the early years, tradition indicated that men would sit on one side of the sanctuary and women and children on the opposite side. The services were delivered in Swedish. Under the leadership of Rev. Theodore J. Paulson every other service was delivered in English beginning in 1931.

At Frank Lake Covenant, pastors served the church from 1877 through 1985, when the church eventually closed its doors. The early pastors were immigrants from Sweden.

All the pastors of Frank Lake Covenant invested time and energy to keep the church in well-working order.

Many descriptions and reports gave indication as to each pastor's giftings, but as per the sadness of history, unfortunately, several pastors were not described in the annals of time.

A list of the pastors who served at the church from 1877 through 1985 is included. Highlights of a few of the eighteen pastors and photos of a number of other pastors who served at Frank Lake Covenant Church are on the following pages.

❧ The Pastors of Frank Lake Covenant Church ☙

1877-1885	Rev. Charles Magnus Youngquist, wife Emma (pioneer vision caster)
1885-1890	Rev. A. Sundberg (advocate of the vision)
1890-1905	Rev. Nils (Larsson) Frykman, wife Betty (musical composer, strong leader)
1905-1912	Rev. Theodore Steinert, wife Alma (peacemaker)
1912-1917	Rev. Adolph William Carlson, wife Anna Charlotte Larson (strong leader)
1917-1919	Rev. Arvid Jacob 'AJ' Ostling, wife Ester (farmer/musician, aggressive)
1919-1921	Student Pastors (names unknown)
1921-1923	Rev. Lars B. Challman, wife Hannah
1923-1926	Rev. Sven Emil (Josefsson) Roslin, wife Christine
1926-1931	Rev. Theodore J. Paulson, wife Amanda (brought English into Sunday services)
1931-1933	Rev. Martin Reinertson
1933-1937	Rev. Ervil Gustafson, wife Helen
1937-1939	No permanent pastor (served by Rev. C. D. Anderson, Willmar Covenant)
1939-1943	Rev. Albin E. Nelson, wife Violet (patient/scholar)
1944-1945	Rev. Able Bloom, wife Maymie
1945-1952	Rev. Eddie R. Stenlund, wife Myra (diligent)
1953-1959	Rev. Richard Lundgren, wife Marilyn (sense of humor)
1959-1966	Rev. Edwin S. Johnson, wife Viola (carpenter/renovator)
1967-1974	Rev. Dennis Slaathaug, wife Shirley (scholar)
1974-1985	Rev. Reuben Bengtson, wife Marian

REV. CHARLES MAGNUS YOUNGQUIST 1877-1885:

❧ Synodical Conference 1882 ☙
Covenant Pastors ~ Princeton, Illinois, Group

Andrew E. Wenstrand, Andrew Hallner, Carl August Bjork,
Carl Magnus Youngquist ~ First Frank Lake Pastor 1877-1885,
Johan Peter Lindell, C. W. Boquist, C. O. Sahlstrom, J. A. Hultman,
Goran Norsen, P. Wedin, Emanual Berg, E. August Skogsbergh,
J. F. Soderstrom, J. F. Berggren, J. Gustafson, J. Peterson, C. J. Edoff,
J. F. Graberg, N. P. Zakrison, K. A. Johnson

REV. A. SUNDBERG 1885-1890:

❧ Rev. A. Sundberg ✍

REV. NILS (LARSSON) FRYKMAN 1890-1905:

Although each pastor had a significant role to play, one pastor in particular, Nils Frykman, profoundly impacted the history of the Covenant church as a whole, as well as the five little churches that he pastored in rural Minnesota during the years of 1890-1905.

Born in Sweden on October 20, 1842, Nils Larsson was a quiet and studious child. His father died while he was young, leaving the family to struggle against poverty. Nils completed school and entered the state teachers' college in Karlstad, Sweden. When he registered, he adopted the surname Frykman—taken from "Fryksdalen" where he was born.

❧ Rev. Nils Frykman ✍

At age 20, Nils accepted Christ as Savior. After graduation, he obtained a position as a school teacher, and married Betty Johnson, the daughter of a district judge. Betty's father opposed the marriage and never gave his blessing.

Nils began to preach, teach, and write hymns. He served as a school teacher for 15 years and wrote a textbook called *The Christian Faith*, used for catechetical classes in the Swedish Evangelical Mission Covenant Church.

But as Frykman began to follow the 'free church movement' the school board disapproved and threatened to fire him. Nils appealed to Sweden's King Oscar and the king ruled in Nils' favor. However, dissention continued until Nils eventually resigned.

In 1888, Nils immigrated to America. He served as a pastor in Chicago for two years but was voted down at the re-election meeting to serve another year. One woman who was present at the meeting stated:

> I could never forget the sad look on Mr. Frykman's face as he walked out of the church that day. One 'pious' man had even circulated a petition against him, but when the election was over he went around soliciting contributions for a gold watch as a gift for the retiring pastor.

Disheartened at rejection, Nils answered a call from a Scandinavian settlement in Kandiyohi County and left Chicago to serve Salem Mission Covenant, Pennock, Minnesota. In addition, from 1890 to 1905, Nils was circuit pastor for four other churches, including: Frank Lake, Lundby, Lake Florida, and West Lake.

Nils arrived with his wife and nine children on December 20, 1889, and changed the face of rural Minnesota and the Covenant Church forever.

During his lifetime, he wrote approximately 300 hymns for the Covenant Church, including "Joy Bells are Ringing" and "I Have a Friend Who Loveth Me."

A local Swift County resident, Vernie Larson Swenson, wrote this about Frykman in her journal:

> *We awaited his arrival with expectancy and excitement. The house was cleaned and burnished and ordered; we children had been bathed and dressed in clean second best clothes and admonished about manners and conduct. Then we would watch for the first hint of a dot on the horizon which might indicate that Frykman's sleigh or buggy was approaching on the Murdock road. Pastor Frykman never ignored children as older grownups generally did. When at our house, Frykman would spend hours at our piano. He had his special gift: he composed hymns.*

From my studies of 1900's Swift County residents Esther Dahl and Vernie Larson Swenson, both reported how they would eagerly await Nils' arrival, how he enjoyed the lutefisk, but abruptly jumped from the table to the piano, announcing, *"I feel a song coming on."*

In Vernie Larson Swenson's book, *Mrs. Lillington to Mrs. Fairfield*, she described her opinion of the great pastor.

Pastor Nils Frykman; who himself radiated tolerance, love and kindness. The affection in which they held him, even tempered the attitude of the congregation towards each other. My very first conception of God as an entity was merged with the familiar image of Pastor Frykman. So must God look: silky, silvery, abundant hair; full, fluffy, matching sideburns. Loving of expression; gently humorous of speech. Oh yes, that was God, too--glorified of course-seated on a silvery, billowing cloud way up somewhere. But benevolent toward His creatures, His earth children.

Frykman liked to jolly the folk around him. This good humor and sense of humor made people feel easy with him about. I do know that we hang on his every word for his goodness, his sweet and understanding nature. He didn't need to talk of God for us to know that he was of God. He was our link with God.

When at our house, Frykman would spend hours at our piano. He had his special gift: he composed hymns. We could hear him trying out a measure, changing, repeating, until we, too, hummed a melody still in the making. Thus, "Hör du den skallande röst" ("Do You Hear the Ringing Voice") came into being at our house.

❧ One of Frykman's Many Hymns ✍

❧ Rev. Nils Frykman Family ❦

❧ Rev. Nils Frykman & Sons ❦

The occupations of Rev. Nils Frykman's children as recalled by great-grandson, Dr. Richard Carlson:

Andrew 'AT': Covenant minister in Rockford, IL
Anna: Worked for my grandfather, lived with my grandparents, never married
Carl: Electrician/Owner Frykman Electric Company, Minneapolis (my grandfather's partner)
Gust: Worked at NSP (Northern States Power) in Minneapolis
Hilma: Dressmaker
Nathaniel: Studebaker car salesman
Oscar: Electrical inspector in Minneapolis
Otto: Electrical inspector in Detroit, MI
Paul: Worked at Northwestern Bell in Minneapolis
Victor: Electrician/Owner Frykman Electric Company, Minneapolis (my grandfather)

REV. THEODORE STEINERT 1905-1912:

During the days of 1907, when pastors were concerned with getting congregants to church, concerned about finances and the price of grain, the nation as a whole was dealing with larger issues.

The Immigration Act of 1907, the Banker's panic, and fights over women's rights created a troubled feel over the nation.

But in rural Murdock, Rev. Theodore Steinert had many of his own troubles to deal with at Frank Lake Covenant Church.

❧ Rev. Theodore Steinert ☙

The Swift County Monitor reported one of Rev. Steinert's troubles on Friday, March 1, 1907:

A WARNING

At a business meeting held at the Frank Lake Mission Church on Thursday, Feb. 14, 1907, for the purpose of deciding what to do with the gang that disturbed the Christmas festival in the above-mentioned church on the evening of Dec. 25, 1906. It was unanimously decided:

That as parents and relatives of some members of the gang have lately become so bold as to deny that any serious disturbance did occur at and in our church during above mentioned Christmas festival, we hereby declare that a disturbance of a serious and even dangerous kind, actually did occur at the above mentioned festival in and around our church, and that disturbance consisted in yelling, laughing and loud talking inside the church and swearing and drinking and loud yelling outside of the church, but on the church premises.

There were also some in rigs who were driving madly back and forth on the road in front of the church and around the barn on the church premises and also actually driving their horses and buggies up in other people's sleighs, whipping their horses in a most inhumane and cruel manner.

Furthermore, when we had locked the church doors to keep out the gang (and how necessary that was, must be evident when it is known that some of them were so drunk that one of them, a mere boy, actually committed in the hall of the church and refusing to walk out, had to be taken out by force) they filled the key hole with gravel so that when the meeting was over the doors could not be opened with the key, but had to be broken open. What that would have meant in case of fire, and in a church as crowded as ours was then, everyone knows.

Going home the gang kept up its record as human brutes, by scaring peaceful people with their swearing and cursing and even striking people with their horse whips. One of our respectable citizens was struck severely by the whip, but as he was angry with them because of their doings at the church, the toughs got their pay, as we have heard, in fine and memorable manner.

We, as a Christian church, decided that as it is our duty to show kindness and forbearance toward all our enemies as far as this can be done without risking the stability of law and justice in the community, we will not at this time bring the culprits to answer before the law for their doings, but only give them and others who might be like-minded a solemn warning not to repeat these crimes against the laws of God and against the laws of the state of Minnesota, as this will be the last time that any leniency will be shown to disturbers of any of our meetings.

Hence forth, all crimes against order and decency in or about our church premises will be punished to the fullest extent of the law.

Theodore Steinert, Pastor;

Edwin Johnson, Chairman;

Claus Larson, Secretary

In order to build a parsonage, during that same time of leadership from Rev. Theodore Steinert, the congregation purchased four acres of land from John Wass, in 1910. The parsonage was built in the summer of 1911.

❧ Frank Lake Parsonage ❦

REV. ADOLPH WILLIAM CARLSON 1912-1917:

In June of 1912, Rev. A.W. Carlson was called. He and his wife were the first occupants of the new parsonage and made their home there until 1917. The original parsonage remains on the Frank Lake site.

❧ Rev. Adolph & Anna Carlson Family ❦

REV. ARVID JACOB OSTLING 1917-1919:

❧ Rev. Arvid 'AJ' & Ester Ostling Family ☙

In November of 1917, Rev. Arvid Jacob 'AJ' Ostling began his ministry at the Frank Lake Church.

Ostling was a farmer and kept horses, cows, sheep, pigs and chickens at the parsonage.

Because he served West Lake, Buffalo Lake, and Frank Lake congregations, he kept a good strong team of horses for driving purposes. It was eighteen miles to Buffalo Lake and six miles to West Lake.

Rev. Ostling and his wife Ester were both excellent musicians. They worked diligently during the time of their service to foster the musical talents of the young people of the church.

The Frank Lake choir was directed by Pastor Ostling and was known to be outstanding in its time.

❧ Piano Purchased 1917-1919 ❦
Resides Today on the Stage at the Church in the Grove

REV. SVEN EMIL (JOSEFSSON) ROSLIN 1923-1926:

Sven Emil Josefsson was born in Gullerad, Sweden, in 1868. He changed his surname to Roslin when he came to America. Rev. Roslin graduated from the Chicago Theological Seminary in 1899 and served in Chicago until 1903. He then moved to Iowa serving congregations in both Stanton and Boone until he accepted the position at Frank Lake and Buffalo Covenant churches.

During the time that Rev. Roslin was pastoring, the church building received a complete renovation when the main auditorium was redecorated with tin sheeting and the exterior was painted.

❧ Rev. Sven & Christine Roslin Family ☙

REV. MARTIN REINERTSON 1931-1933:

ஃ Rev. Martin Reinertson ஃ

REV. ALBIN E. NELSON 1939-1943:

❧ Rev. Albin E. & Violet Nelson ❧

❧ Confirmation Class ❧
October 5, 1941
Rev. Nelson

REV. EDDIE R. STENLUND 1945-1952:

Rev. Eddie & Myra Stenlund

❧ Confirmation Class ☙
Rev. Stenlund

REV. RICHARD LUNDGREN 1953-1959:

❧ Rev. Richard & Marilyn Lundgren ☙

When Rev. Richard Lundgren was called on January 1, 1953 to serve the Frank Lake and Buffalo Lake churches, he was invited to spend the weekend, conduct services, interview with the call committee and pray about the opportunity. He and his wife Marilyn accepted the call.

But Rev. Lundgren said this about moving his wife and two preschool-age boys to the parsonage:

The parsonage was in serious need of repair and upgrading. There was no running water, no kitchen cupboards and a coal-wood burning furnace that needed hourly attention. It was far from what we had known all our lives living in Minneapolis. But, we were both anxious to serve the Lord. I quit my job in Minneapolis, we packed up leaving behind our comfortable home. The next spring, repair and modernization of the parsonage began.

When asked about the salary in the 1950s, Lundgren said, *I left a much larger salary behind for $200 a month. I received $85 a month from Frank Lake and $115 from Buffalo Lake. Needless to say, our month income was well depleted long before the next month pay arrived. But with free eggs, milk and a few packages of meat along the way, we managed to stay alive and happy in the service of our Lord and Savior.*

Lundgren continued: *90 above or 30 below we had services. When the fuel oil in the outside tank became too cold to flow we could not have a service. A few blizzards cancelled services.*

Midweek Bible study and prayer services were held on Wednesdays at Buffalo Lake and on Thursdays at Frank Lake.

It was on a cold January morning that we climbed into our old 1940 Ford and headed west arriving at the Frank Lake Covenant Church parsonage with its torn and tattered window shades and the little slanted roof shanty out in the back yard.

Two young kids just anxious to serve the Lord whatever the inconveniences and the future might hold. God is good!

REV. EDWIN S. JOHNSON 1959-1966

❧ Confirmation Class ☙
Rev. Johnson

❧ Merry Forsell Netland Wedding ❧
September 24, 1966

Rev. Youngquist may have been the first pastor and Rev. Bengtson the last, but along with the other pastors they had incredible faith. No matter the cost, no matter the physical surroundings, the men who were called to serve the circuit churches stepped up to the call of the Almighty.

Each one came from his own little world, where things may or may not have been easier. They arrived in their horse and buggies, or their old cars, but nevertheless, they arrived and settled in for however long the Lord needed them to serve.

Various calls to other churches, illnesses or circumstances that led them away may have taken charge of the pastor's world, but life of service continued on for each one of them.

The life of Frank Lake Covenant and those who attended was forever shaped and molded by the words, the shepherds' hearts, and the actions of each man listed on these pages. They gave it everything they had to serve God.

In the end, their story is never forgotten for it continues to live on ...

We will reap the harvest because they did not give up.

A Visit to a Country Church
By Wilhamine Huber

It's just a little country church,
Beside a country road,
The weathered gravestones lean a bit
But the grass is always mowed.

The old bell up in the steeple
is silent forever more,
And to hinder the aimless vagabond
There's a padlock on the door.

What stories the old church could tell
If it could only speak
Of pioneers who weathered odds,
And worshipped here each week.

They're resting now in the church yard,
Sheltered by the oaks
And the cities with their modern ways,
Have enticed the younger folks.

Vast changes are the way of things
As through this life we pass,
And the old church is now deserted,
Except for someone who mows the grass.

☙ *Written on August 23, 1987, after stopping at the Frank Lake Covenant Church north of Murdock, MN. This is the church where my mother, Winnie Hallberg, attended Sunday school and was confirmed. As the poem tells, the church is no longer in use and it was locked securely. But it was very noticeable that the grounds are still lovingly cared for.*

☙ *Wilhamine sent me this poem in 2012 and gave me permission to use the poem in this book. She went home to the Lord in 2013.*

❧ The People ❧

Which He commanded our fathers that they should teach them (the statutes) to their children,
that the generation to come might know, even the children yet to be born,
that they may arise and tell them to their children.
Psalm 78:5b-6

So often in life, it's easy to believe that we don't matter, that we have no earthly purpose, no eternal one. After all, how could one life make a difference upon an entire world? Or how could one simplistic life, out in the middle of nowhere, impact future generations?

Looking back at the lives that made up the congregation of Frank Lake Covenant Church from the late 1800s to 1980, many of those lives were intertwined with each other. Whether it was through the relationships of family, marriage, or neighbors, one life truly did impact another.

On a bright and sunny spring day, I took a trip and rode over the back roads of the farming community that surrounded the original site of the little white church. My tour guide, Marlene Carlson Hauge, was a lovely member of the Frank Lake Church from the 1940s. Her family had attended the church and she knew every farm and every uncle, aunt, and cousin who had driven their old Fords to the church on Sunday mornings.

I was mesmerized by the beautiful scenery of wide open fields of grain, thick groves of trees and various old farm homes, some abandoned, some updated. My soul ached to be able to catch a glimpse of them back in time, observing the farmers out on their tractors and the wives hanging laundry on the clothesline. Little children would be gathering eggs and helping with chores, all the while preparing to head to Frank Lake Covenant that next Sunday morning.

But alas, all I spotted was one old black lab tottering towards the mailbox, too tired to bark, and a few flittering birds flying over the broken down clothesline.

Marlene chatted away, filling me in on the relationships between farms. When we drove up to one towering old home, she stayed at the end of the driveway. I could see the reflection in her eyes and noticed the same yearning for a page to turn back in time so we could see it as it once was … yesterday.

Yesterday, from 1875-1960, the church was the center of your world, whether you lived in town or in the country. It became the one essential thing that brought focus to your family and to your well-being.

Marlene remembered:

As a little girl, I would come to this farm with my mother. In those days, these people were considered very wealthy. They had special dishes that they would bring out for the coffee time. I loved to look around at the beautiful curtains and furniture.

Swaying now in the breeze was some white, flimsy curtain, blowing against some apparatus that allowed cable access. She sighed out loud and the moment was gone.

She continued to share:

In our family, there was no excuse to not be at church ... it was just automatic that you went to every service.

If you had speakers there at church that day, you'd invite them home for dinner after Sunday services. A typical Sunday yielded about fifty people. The majority of those people at your church were your social group. Those are the people you saw, did things with, and knew everything about.

1958 Confirmation

Back: Vickie Mattson
Kathy Johnson
Marlene Carlson
Merry Forsell

Front: Roseann Neal
Rev. Lundgren
Gary Olson

The families that lived around Frank Lake and the Murdock area supported the church, supported their pastors and supported each other. That's what people did. There was time for helping neighbors when they were in trouble. Mothers and fathers would not tolerate laziness, back talk, or disrespect to themselves or others. People put God first without question.

While perusing the roads of a ten-mile radius around the church, I listened to the names of neighbors she recited and realized that most, if not all, were of Swedish descent. They included: Bergstroms, Olaf Carlson, Reynold and Juliet Carlson, Dahls, Felts, Charles and Augusta Forsell, Oscar and Pearl Forsell, Hallbergs, Roy and Elsie Hookenson, Johnsons, Howard and Violet 'Vye' Larson, Mellgrens, Olsons, Sands, Turnquists, and the Wennerbergs.

Church records stated that in 1914, membership was at 46 people, but by 1948, membership had dropped to 24 people. However, Pastor Lundgren, who served in the 1950s, stated that he remembered the services always being full. The little church comfortably sat 100 people.

Each family in attendance contributed financially as they could afford, but they also supported their pastors with much-needed garden produce, along with eggs and meat. Many families raised their children in the church and felt an incredible sense of pride as they watched them learn about Christ and become confirmed.

Some of the attendees throughout the early years of the church:

Olaus Olsen Berg:

Olaus was born September 22, 1834. He was married to Maria Christina Berg, born September 28, 1834. Olaus, known in Frank Lake's records as "O. O. Berg" served on the first board of the church and was also a deacon.

His daughter, Emma, had Vernie Larson Swenson. Another daughter, Elizabeth, was the mother of Mamie Falk.

Olaus served the church diligently and filled in with preaching and teaching when the circuit pastors were unable to be at the church.

In Vernie Larson Swenson's book, *Mrs. Lillington to Mrs. Fairfield,* she wrote this about her grandpa:

> *These were still circuit rider days, when, with no resident pastor, there were more Sundays without a preacher than with one. An ordained preacher that is; our Grandpa Berg was a lay preacher who filled in adequately and eagerly; who also was authorized to baptize and to marry and to bury, should such need arise.*

Joseph Carlson:

Joseph was the son of Olaf and Emma Carlson. It was rumored that Joseph rode his motorcycle outside of the church while service was taking place. He got in big trouble.

Olaf and Emma Carlson:

Olaf and Emma emigrated from Sweden in 1892. The Carlson family attended the church in the early 1900s.

Olaf served as janitor for the building and grounds.

Joseph Carlson

Olaf & Emma Carlson

Anna Alfreda 'Freda' Dahl Larson:

Anna, known as Freda, married Harry Larson from Rockford, Illinois. Freda served as the Frank Lake Covenant organist during the early 1900s. It was noted in her sister Esther's journal that she was nervous about what songs Rev. Nils Frykman would choose for the service. Freda died a few days after giving birth to her daughter, Marion Larson, from pneumonia brought on by a raging flu in 1920.

❧ Esther Teaching Children ❦

❧ Freda Larson ❦

Charles and Christina Dahl:

Charles and Christina moved to Hayes Township, Swift County, Murdock, Minnesota, in 1904. They attended the church with their seven children from 1904-1924. They made the church and its activities the center of their everyday world.

From a journal I read, written by Esther Dahl, Charles and Christina's daughter, I learned how the family traveled between Kerkhoven, Benson, and Willmar, buying and selling pigs and eggs, and purchasing pieces of fabric to sew.

The journal described the community of neighbors as they went to church Sundays and Wednesdays, ate together after meetings, participated in various clubs that supported the church and loved and served God.

When I spoke with Denny Thompson, great-grandson of Charles and Christina, he said:

> From 1920-1930 my mother lived on her grandparents farm (Charles and Christina Dahl) just southeast of the Frank Lake Church. Her mother, Freda Dahl, had played the church organ there. Esther Forsell, who led the choir for many years, was my mother's cousin.
>
> A Rev. Carlson who served at the church was married to Anna Larson Carlson. When her brother, Harry Larson, came from Rockford, Illinois, to visit the Frank Lake Church he met my grandmother Freda Dahl. They married and moved to Rockford.
>
> Freda died in 1920 two weeks after my mom, Marion Larson Thompson, was born. Freda's sister, Emma Dahl Chryst, took my mom to the Frank Lake farm and they lived there until her grandfather Charles Dahl passed away in 1930.
>
> Charles and Christina's son, Rueben, attended North Park Seminary (Covenant School) and became a Covenant pastor. His roommate Benjie (Immanuel but nicknamed Benjie because his last name was Franklin) went home to visit his family at Frank Lake. Benjie met Adla Dahl (another child of Charles and Christina's) and they got married. Benjie became a Covenant pastor.
>
> Mom wrote in her journal that much of the Dahl life revolved around the church. Their faith has influenced six generations of our family since that time.
>
> Mom taught piano lessons for 40 years. She passed away on Christmas Eve 2008 after enjoying a Swedish Christmas celebration at our home and playing the piano for all of us. All of our children play the piano and have served as worship leaders in various churches.

❧ Dahl's New Home ☙

Back: Carl 'Charles', Anna 'Freda', Emma, Mable Christina

Front: Axel, Adla, Carl 'Rueben' Esther

Charles & Christina Dahl Family

Back: Mable, Rueben, Emma, Freda, Adla, Axel, Esther

Front: Charles & Christina

Mamie Anderson Falk Bergstrom:

Born in 1896 to the Swedish immigrants Mr. and Mrs. A. J. Anderson, Mamie was next to the youngest of nine children and was raised on the family farm near Frank Lake. Olaus Olsen Berg was her grandfather (deacon and first chairman of the church board).

She studied music at the Agricultural School in Morris, Minnesota, and at the Minnehaha Academy in Minneapolis, Minnesota.

Self-taught, Mamie eventually became an accomplished portrait and landscape artist. She began painting in the 1940s, but really intensified her efforts in the 1950s, and her career took off when her grandchildren were small.

In an interview with the *Swift County Monitor*, Mamie said, *"I tried to tell them stories of the early days of the pioneers. I started to paint to illustrate to them that way of life."*

Falk indicated she just wanted to recall the days of pioneer life on the beautiful, but often harsh, Minnesota prairie.

Mamie Anderson and her husband, August Falk, were married at Frank Lake Covenant, Murdock, on November 30, 1917.

❧ Mamie Anderson Falk ❦

Mamie painted the Frank Lake Covenant church in the background of her painting entitled, *Music Lesson Days*. A copy of this painting is at Frank Lake church today, along with her original painting of Rev. Nils Frykman. Here is what she said about memories that prompted that specific painting:

> *My piano lessons were an all day project. It took three hours for my father to take me the nine miles into town. We rode in either a top buggy, carriage or wagon with a load of grain, depending on the time of year. In town, I would catch the 1:00 p.m. train to the neighboring town, four miles away. Following the lesson, I would reverse the process and with luck arrive home before dark.*

Music Lesson Days ~ Frank Lake Church in Background

In 1976, Mamie's paintings were the subject of a television documentary produced in Sweden by the Sweden Television Network.

Mamie's nephew, Richard Falk, said this about his aunt:

> When she first started painting, she'd sell them for $10-12. I just wasn't interested in them and didn't particularly like them. But one day I was in Minneapolis for a sale at Elaine's Gallery and three of Mamie's paintings sold for over 10k. She was a very gifted and charming lady. Not just with art, but with her music and their family life. She was a devoted mother.

At one point, Mamie donated seven of her pioneer works to The House of Emigrants in Växjö, Sweden, for an exhibit. Two of Mamie's paintings are hanging in the office of the deputy director of the Smithsonian Institute.

Charles G. and Augusta Forsell:

Charles Forsell was born in Ostergotland, Sweden, in 1866. He learned to be a blacksmith by trade and immigrated to America in 1885.

Charles and Augusta were farmers who came from Chicago, Illinois. Charles's first wife, Olivia, died in 1902 and left behind their two young boys. Olivia asked him to have her friend Augusta Johnson, born in 1863, take care of her boys.

Charles and Augusta were married in 1903 and moved to a farm close to Augusta's sister, Christina Dahl, in 1904, and lived near the Frank Lake church in rural Swift County.

Forsell's daughter with Augusta, Esther, led the famous Frank Lake choir and created a strong force of musicians who would produce an album. Charles was widowed again in 1930.

Both are buried in the family plot at Frank Lake Church Cemetery.

❧ Charles & Augusta Forsell ☙

Winnie Violet Hallberg:

Winnie attended Frank Lake Covenant in 1897 through 1917, with her parents and siblings, until they moved to New London, Minnesota. She was confirmed at the church. Her parents, Emil and Anna, had seven children and were farmers in the rural Murdock area.

Winnie married Clarence Johnson and had Wilhamine Johnson Huber and Pearl Johnson. Wilhamine was named after "a wonderful piano teacher whom her mother loved and thought the name was pretty."

Esther Forsell Johnson:

Esther was married to Raymond Johnson and lived near the Frank Lake Church. Raymond's father, Ernest Johnson, was the "burly" man who saved the organ from the original church that burned. Ernest was a brother to Dennis Johnson's *(the man who sold us the church)* grandfather.

A school teacher by profession, Esther was the organist for Frank Lake for forty-five years and played hymns on the rescued organ.

Esther served the church well as choir director. She organized a Swedish choir where the children at the church who did not know Swedish, learned the hymns phonetically.

Esther described the origin of the Midsommar Festival in the *Kerkhoven Banner* published at the time:

The idea of recreating a Midsommar Festival came when I heard the song "Sjung den Igen" ("Sing It Again") sung by an obviously non-Swedish television star. If she could learn the foreign lyrics, surely the youth of our community could learn them also. The plan was presented to a committee and was somewhat skeptically accepted. Thus, the Frank Lake Swedish chorus was born.

❧ Esther & Raymond Johnson ☙

Documents indicate that old hymnals were found in the attic and songs were chosen. The teenagers and adults alike were excited with the idea. The meaning of each hymn's line was carefully learned.

The Swedish Midsommar Festival was held in June of 1961. The little church was filled to capacity again in 1962 for the second annual festival which featured the youth groups and Sunday school of the church.

Esther's description of the event was published in the *Kerkhoven Banner* and included this statement:

> *Even persons who do not understand the Swedish language enjoyed the festival very much. The kindest compliments came from them.*

The program included many hymns such as:

"Tryggare Kan Ingen Vara"
("Children of the Heavenly Father"),
"Nere I Dalen" ("Down in the Valley"),
"Barnen For Jesus" ("The Children For Jesus"),
and "Snart ar jag Hemma" ("Soon I'll be at Home").

When the Swedish choir recorded the album *Midsommars Fest: i Frank Lake Kyrkan* (In the Frank Lake Church) in 1965 at the church, the people were enthralled with the album.

❧ Esther Forsell Johnson ☙
Inspired to Record a Swedish Album with Members of the Frank Lake Choir

The music was aired on WCCO radio in the Twin Cities. A description of the record on the back of the album stated:

> *Transported from Sweden, staunch and strong in their new found faith resulting from the "great revival" in the early eighties; our forefathers sang the songs of hope and cheer that have become our spiritual heritage. Our program of Swedish songs was dedicated to the memory of these pioneers of faith, who with diligence, fortitude, and sacrifice carved a Christian community in the uncompromising wilderness of the prairie.*

Marie Johnson, wife of Dennis Johnson, an alto vocalist on the production remembered:

> *I know while the recording was going on we had to stop as a tractor with a piece of machinery was driving by. Suppose maybe the windows were open because it was summer. Sort of surprising that the recording can be as good as it is being made in those conditions.*

Members of the chorus in 1966-67 that made the album were:

    Michelle Applegren
    Bonnie Falk
    Evelyn Felt
    Eldon Felt
    Charlotte Forsell
    Janet Holmberg
    Jeanne Holmberg
    Albert Johnson
    Dennis Johnson
    Diane Johnson
    Dorothy Johnson
    Helen Johnson
    Kathleen Johnson
    Marie Johnson
    Richard Johnson
    Ronald Johnson
    Dianne Larson
    Jennifer Larson
    Mary Ellen Lindell
    Susan Magnuson
    Ardell Nelson
    Janice Olson

❧ Open Church Windows ☙

❦ Midsommars Fest Album Front Cover 1965 ❦

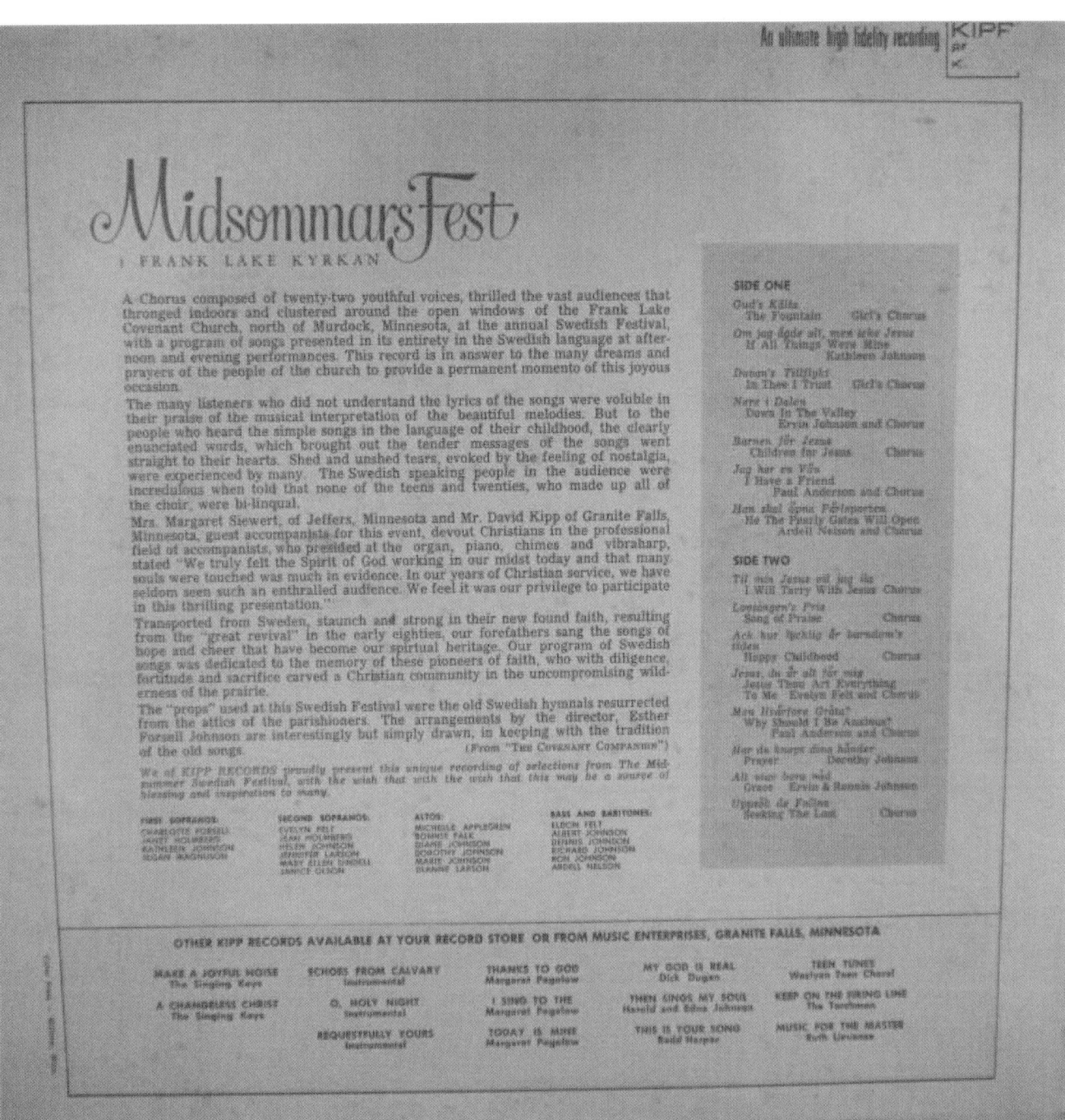

🌿 Midsommars Fest Album Back Cover 1965 🌿

Ervin Johnson:

Ervin Johnson was born in 1910 to farmers Edwin and Amanda Johnson. He married Nina Felt and farmed his family's property close to the Frank Lake Covenant Church. His father and uncle were very devoted to serving the church. Ervin served as church treasurer on the executive board for Frank Lake in 1948.

Ervin's son, Dennis Johnson (wife Marie) was a member of the Hillside Cemetery Association that took care of the gravesites at the property. In 2012, the Association determined to sell the church building for $1.00 on Craigslist. Dennis and Marie spearheaded the sale to Dean and Kathy Weckwerth on May 8, 2012.

Confirmation Class 1926
Back: Marlin (Last name unknown), Reynold Carlson, Marvin Dahl, Clarence Carlson, Oscar Forsell, (Name not included), Ervin Johnson, Raymond Johnson
Front: Evelyn Larson, Hattie Anderson, Rev. Roslin, Esther Forsell, Alice Palm, Marie Palm
(All Confirmands from Frank Lake Covenant Church)

❧ Confirmation Class *circa* 1951 ❦

Back: Laura Turnquist, Carol Larson, Carol Stenlund, Donald Carlson, Dennis Johnson
(Members from Frank Lake Covenant Church)

Middle: Lavilla Neal, Clarence Neal Jr., Unknown Mattson
Front: Walter Clark, Rev. Eddie Stenlund, Unknown Mattson
(Members from Buffalo Lake Covenant Church)

Rev. Stenlund pastored both churches.

Andrew Johan Jonasson:
(Later called Andrew John Anderson)

In 1866, at age fourteen, Andrew emigrated from Sweden with his parents Jonas and Katherine. They traveled in a covered wagon to Princeton, Illinois. In Princeton, Andrew lost his mother, sister, and aunt to cholera. Andrew, his father and one remaining sister settled in Waseca, Minnesota.

In 1871, Jonas remarried and he and Andrew established homesteads in 1873 near Frank Lake, seven miles north of Murdock, Minnesota.

Andrew was married on June 9, 1877, in Waseca, Minnesota, to Elizabeth "Lizzy" Christine Berg, daughter of O.O. Berg. They were the parents of Mamie Falk, the painter.

Andrew was one of the original members (died in 1912) of Frank Lake Swedish Mission Church. Rev. Carlson delivered the funeral service.

Charles and Augusta Johnson (Carl Jonasson):

Carl Jonasson (Charles Johnson) and his wife, Augusta, were married in 1864 and settled in Kerkhoven in 1876 with their nine young children. In 1877 Charles and Augusta traveled by covered wagon and oxen to live near Frank Lake.

Charles was a religious and community-minded individual and served as one of the charter members of Frank Lake Covenant Church.

Lars Peter Larson:

Lars Peter Larson was born in Jonkoping, Sweden, in 1850. In 1876, he married Sophia Anderson of Jonkoping. They are the parents of a son, Thure. In 1880 the family immigrated to the United States.

The family traveled to Western Minnesota to look for farm land. First the Larsons lived in a sod hut near Frank Lake. Later they obtained land from the railroader, James J. Hill, and continued to live seven miles north of Murdock.

Lars was one of the founders of the Frank Lake Covenant Church.

❧ Jonas Anderson ❧
Andrew Anderson's Father

Esther Moberg:

Although Esther and her family attended Buffalo Lake Covenant Church, Esther's five-year diary revealed that she spent a great amount of time at Frank Lake Covenant due to the fact that both churches were part of the five circuit Covenant churches in the area.

Esther and her siblings, Tena, Amy, Martin and Alf, were very diligent servants to God's work. They constantly supported Frank Lake's events and went to many of the special meetings and picnics.

They loved to serve the pastors by giving them rides, providing meals, helping with Sunday school and Christmas programs, and cleaning the buildings. Esther was well-known as a Sunday school teacher and stayed single her entire life, focusing on taking care of her mother and serving God.

Esther Moberg & Her Sister Amy

Charles Oscar and Emma Adelia (Bergstrom) Sands:

∾

Charles Sands
&
Emma Bergstrom

June 24, 1913
Wedding at Frank Lake
Covenant Church

∾

Charles and Emma's son Luverne, an 85-year-old retired Covenant pastor, visited the newly moved church and told me:

> In the early 1900s, Charles attended a Christian vo-tech school called Willmar Seminary. During that time, a friend who attended the same school, William Bergstrom, invited him home to Murdock for the weekend. While spending the weekend together, Charles met William's sister, the lovely Emma. It was true love.

On June 24, 1913, Charles Sands, 25, and Emma Bergstrom, 21, married at Frank Lake Covenant Church. The Reverend A. W. Carlson officiated.

The Sands were farmers and lived on the outskirts of Eagle Lake near Willmar. Charles and Emma had nine children: Muriel, Winfield, Virgil, Harlie, Donald, Dorothy, Dewey, James and Luverne. Five of their sons served in the military in World War II.

Luverne continued:

> *Every time we visit Minnesota we also visit the cemetery and the farm home that still exists near Frank Lake. Emma's father's name, L. Bergstrom, County Commissioner, is on the 1897 cornerstone of the Swift County Courthouse in Benson, Minnesota.*
>
> *Mother moved after marriage to the Willmar area and most of her siblings moved to Montana. Her brother became Warden of the state penitentiary in Missoula, Montana.*
>
> *One of the Frykman brothers (Nils) was a hymn writer and while he preached in my mother's church was often invited to Axel Bergstrom's home for Sunday dinner. My mother remembers him excusing himself from the dinner table by saying, "I feel a song coming on," and he would go to the piano and work on that song in her home.*
>
> *Mamie Falk's second marriage (11/22/1962) was to my mother's brother (my uncle), William 'Bill' Bergstrom.*

Three of the Sand's children, Donald, Dewey, and Luverne, went on to become Covenant pastors.

Vernie Larson Swenson:

Vernie Larson was born in 1894 to Claus and Emma Larson. She was a first cousin to Mamie Falk and a first cousin of Ervin Johnson. She was another granddaughter of Olaus Olson Berg. Vernie was married to George Swenson.

In 1966, Vernie Larson Swenson began to write her memories of a child growing up on a farm near the Frank Lake Covenant church. It was written from the vantage point of a young girl of thirteen. She entitled it *Mrs. Lillington to Mrs. Fairfield*, since she and her sister Ethel had assumed these grown-up names in their playtime. The book was also known as *Small Kettles* which referred to the Swedish saying "Small kettles also have big ears," meaning the girls picked up information not intended for them.

Vernie's book described the experience she had at age twelve when she started *läsa för prästen* (ready for the priest), which led to confirmation.

Vernie wrote:

I found the weekly Saturday-forenoon sessions altogether enjoyable; the extra occasion of being with my friends, the getting better acquainted with such boys and girls as came only to our Sunday school—not to District 40 West; the making friends with the few who joined with us from the West Lake Church.

I enjoyed thoroughly, the study assignments: the long chapters we must read; the continuous questions we must ponder; the answers in the Catechism to be learned verbatim.

I enjoyed, as well, helping Kelly with our lessons—for he did not take happily to reading and memorizing Swedish and our cutter rides, those wintry months, the two miles to church.

If only this had been in the days of Pastor Frykman then all would have been wonderful. With Pastor Steinert we hadn't yet got used to him nor could we feel at ease with him.

❧ Vernie Larson Swenson ❦

These are but a few of the many families that were members of Frank Lake Covenant. And throughout warm sunny summer days, wintry storms, and bitter Minnesota blizzards, the farmers and their families made their way to the church, worshipped together, and it made them stronger.

The very core of their being was striving to be their best amidst adverse challenges. And in the archives and journals that I discovered from the late 1800s to the 1950s, there were no questions as to whether or not their lives would matter ...

They just lived their faith,

Taught their children about God,

&

Believed that was what mattered.

The Search

Many are the plans in a person's heart
But it's the Lord's purpose that prevails.
Proverbs 19:21

I remember the day that I traveled home from the Twin Cities. It was dark and rainy and felt much the same as my own weary soul. The rain was dripping down against the windshield as my tears dripped down against my face.

Hours before, my three girls and I had stood in a circle holding hands. My middle child boldly stated, "Mom, whatever happens we agree right now, okay? We are trusting God to overtake the situation. Whatever happens is His will and we will follow Him and then let go. Alright?"

I looked her in the eye, nodding my head yes, and remembered back to the horrible day one year before when my daughter Chandra had been violently attacked by her father, an addict, during one of his fits of anger. At one point, she said the room became black as she was losing consciousness. A mere twenty-one year old, she cried out to God, to let Him know she was ready to leave this world if it was her time to go.

The case had been passed over by the city's police, stating it was her word against that of her father and his girlfriend. When I called the station to argue that undeniably she had been attacked the police officer laughed and mocked me. He stated, "It's their word against hers and she doesn't stand a chance. Just let go of it, will you?"

I remember saying to him, "Sir, do you have any children?"

"No," he answered flatly.

"Then you would have no idea what it feels like to have one of them almost killed, let alone have it happen to them by their parent."

His response, "There's nothing more to be done."

I was driving my car while talking with him and I remember my hands trembled as I clutched the wheel.

"Oh, but there is so much more to be done!" I emphatically stated. "You see, I believe in a God that supersedes over sin that humans bring upon each other. He resides over vengeance and recompense. He is a God of justice and He is my God. I will begin to pray now and you mark my words, one day this will go to court."

The officer laughed. Yes, he laughed at me and said, "You do that," and he hung up the phone.

Under some very unusual circumstances such as God continually uses through history, a short week later, my oldest daughter, who had never received a speeding ticket, was picked up in that same city.

She marched into the courthouse to argue the speeding ticket she received and sat down next to a man dressed in a business suit and tie. He smiled and said, "How are you doing today?"

My child responded, "Oh, I'm here for my first speeding ticket, but that's not really what's bothering me. Mostly I'm upset because a few weeks ago, right here in this city, my sister was violently attacked by my drug-addict father and almost killed. But the police here won't do anything about it."

The man looked shocked. And then something strange happened. He held out his hand and said, "Hi, I'm the city attorney. Let's do something about what happened." So the case went to court. And there was God ... doing what God does ... righting the wrongs.

During the hours of litigating, my child's father had worked diligently to try to disprove what had happened. If only I had notified the police throughout the years of abuse and let them know about his drug addiction, his buying and selling of drugs, and all that we'd been through, they would have had a paper trail. But alas, I was the typical spouse in a co-dependent relationship, married to an abuser.

The judge ordered one-year probation with a mandatory drug test where we would not know the results. I questioned why, but didn't receive a competent answer.

In my anger, I remember falling to the floor and crying. But my children pulled me up and said, "No, we trust God. We cannot argue with His decision. There is a reason for this and someday we may understand. But today, in our confusion, we move forward and go with God.

Go with God, I thought. I was driving now, but my mind was blurry. Where exactly was God going? About twenty miles from home, I drove through Pennock, Minnesota, and a ray of light streamed through the dark rain, washing over my car and flooding light upon me.

In a split second, I realized that God was getting my attention.

I used all of that stored up anger and resentment to propel me towards a different place on the journey of my life.

There, in the seconds of bright light, I cried out to God, "I want to do something different now, God. No more being on staff as a worship director. Instead, I want to help women. I want to help women understand who they're marrying and make the best choices. I want them to learn about God-His Word, His truth, and His desires for them so they can become the very best version of themselves. I want to make a difference with what I now know."

And in those moments, in that darkness, through that ray of light, my life was changed forever.

In the following weeks, I began to work diligently through prayer and seeking God. I began to feel the Holy Spirit revealing to me the future He had prepared for me and I began to walk into it.

This future plan would never have been one that I would have chosen for myself. But in God's wisdom, He was making something good out of something evil that had happened to us.

I remember sitting at my desk at the church and wondering how it would all unfold. I loved my job so very much, but God was moving me out of it now. As my kids had proposed, "We agree to follow Him."

It was early in my prayer and direction-seeking that God put a spotlight on the verse John 10:10. The second half of the verse stuck out to me as I read it quietly, all the while a small stream of sunlight shone in on my desk while a gentle rain was falling outside my office. It seemed somehow connected to the rainy night I had heard from God. I read the words, *I came so they can have real and eternal life, more and better life than they ever dreamed of.*

I knew what God had done throughout my life and I believed that He didn't just want us to live a better life ... but His desire was that we were to live our *BEST LIFE*. I knew in those moments that this would be the name of the women's ministry God was calling me to create ... Best Life Ministries. The purpose statement would be "to create help, hope, and healing by bringing the knowledge of Christ to the hearts and minds of women everywhere."

In the quiet moments when I heard the Spirit talking and prompting, I made a list of the people who I had met along the way on my journey. Women who were everyday people, real and authentic, who had a story to share, who would bring motivation and encouragement, and I called them. One by one they excitedly agreed to get on the bus that was traveling from hurt and abuse, *to help, hope and healing.*

The church where I was serving was not able to promote the ministry and I quickly accepted a job in a neighboring town with a church who agreed to hire me 90% time as a worship director and 10% as Executive Director of Best Life Ministries.

I stayed at that church for the next two years, learning and soaking in everything I could about women's ministry. After a new pastor arrived, I resigned and began giving 100% as Founder and Executive Director of Best Life Ministries.

The early years were difficult. There were days without speaking engagements, months without women's conferences, months without a salary for me and small pay for speakers and musicians. But God was in it and things were happening.

When we spoke, we saw women's lives being changed. The more we did, the more God blessed us. The more God blessed us, the busier we became. The busier we became, the more I realized that in order to move to the next step of really becoming a full-fledged ministry, I believed we needed to find a place to call home, a place for a headquarters.

After the second year, I began to look out at the old Cashel Township schoolhouse across from our home on Minnesota Highway 29. I would look at it and pray and say to God, "Should we talk to them about buying this building for headquarters?" I would always get the same response from the Spirit, "Not yet."

Another year went by and I had prayed the same prayer over and over and received the same answer. Until a warm spring day when I looked out my window at the schoolhouse and prayed my prayer and felt the Spirit of God said, "Go now!" I quickly called and set up a meeting with the Cashel Township Board.

Next, I agreed to a neighborhood coffee where I shared my vision for a headquarters for the ministry that would include Bible studies, monthly get-togethers, and teaching God's Word. I met with my two friends, Mona Young and JaVonne Frentzel, women who'd lived in the neighborhood all of their seventy plus years. As I cast my vision, they encouraged me along.

A week later, I met with Mona Young and her sister-in-law, LuElla Young, and cast a vision for Best Life Ministries. LuElla then shared it with her farmer-husband Donald.

My husband, Dean, and I called our farmer-neighbor LuVerne Bangsund, and asked if we could meet LuVerne and his wife Mona at our home for coffee. With LuVerne 'Vernie' on the township board, we thought we'd get a head start on casting our vision.

When the Bangsunds arrived, I shared the story of the brutal attack on my child, the beginnings of Best Life Ministries, and now our desire to move forward to the next step in the ministry … a headquarters. Vernie was thoroughly excited and encouraged us to meet with the board.

I had been in the old school building a couple of times before and knew that my mother-in-law, now in her eighties, had attended school there, as had my husband and his siblings.

On a warm Tuesday night, filled with utter excitement, Dean and I walked hand-in-hand across the highway to the little building that I thought would become ours. Once inside, I did not feel God's presence. I did not feel He was encouraging me. I felt it was a 'no.' What I didn't understand was the 'why.'

The board members listened to my vision and gently pushed back. Their excuses were presented—there was no bathroom, they used the building a few times a year, and they stored road equipment on the property.

Normally, I would have challenged back, but without the feeling of the pleasure of God, I couldn't say anything but nod and thank them. Defeated, discouraged, confused and yet still challenged, we walked hand-in-hand to our home. We discussed the meeting and I called the neighbors to pray.

A week went by and then another. We set up a meeting with a realtor in the neighboring community of Montevideo, Minnesota, some twenty miles from our home.

I remember the evening well. It was hot and muggy as we went from building to building. One was an old grocery store that had ceiling tiles busted and hanging down across the entire building. Smells of mold and mildew made their way straight for our nostrils. I felt let down and Dean felt dizzy from the smells.

Another was down on the main street of town and consisted of one big open room originally used for a store. Yet another was an old building that had flooring missing, windows broken, and birds flying about. Each property was listed at $800-1400 a month for rent. Nothing was a fit. Nothing was affordable. Nothing would work.

Next, I called the City Manager of Benson, Minnesota, and chatted with him about available spaces. He offered the basement of the bank, the upstairs of the hospital, fire hall, city hall, and an old sanctuary that was tiny and would be shared with another nonprofit.

Once again, discouragement set in and I wanted to give up. My sweet husband, having the farmer mentality that he did, said to me, "We're not renting, we're buying." But where could we find a building to buy and how could we afford it?

I remember a few nights after the phone conversation with the Benson City Manager that I received a call from our neighbor, Donald Young. He and LuElla had been praying for us and he said, "I think you should look for an old church. There's one down the highway and it's for sale." We drove by it, but the old church had been remodeled into a house. I didn't feel it was a fit.

A few days later on a Tuesday morning, Vernie called. He said, "I've been praying about it and I think you should look for an old church to be the headquarters of your ministry."

Again we heard the same answer to our same prayer. Dean and I looked at each other dumbfounded. I said, "Dean, you've lived here your whole life, where is there a church for sale?"

He shook his head because he had no idea. He said, "We could never afford a church building, Kathy. What would it cost, eighty thousand dollars? One hundred forty thousand? Whatever it is, we don't have that kind of money."

That same Tuesday evening, April 24, 2012, I prayed out loud as Dean drove the ten miles home from a Benson restaurant. I prayed for wisdom, insight, direction, revival, and for God to provide a building for the ministry.

The next morning arrived bright and sunny. At 8:00 a.m. my husband called me from his job in town. He said the words I will never forget, "Ma'am, you'll never believe it! You'll never believe what's on the front cover of the Willmar paper!!!"

"What? What?" I questioned.

"A church for sale! It's about twenty miles from our house." Dean said.

"How much is it?" I asked breathlessly.

"One dollar! You better get up there and look at it, quick! Before somebody else buys it!" Dean instructed.

And so I did. I threw my sandals on my feet, grabbed my purse and keys and began to head for the door when the phone rang. It was the voice of Vernie shouting in my ear and saying, "Did you see it! Did you see it! A church for one dollar!"

I told Vernie I was on my way up to see the church.

For years I had a specific prayer. It was a prayer that included my heart's desires. I wanted to work for the ministry full-time and not worry about how God would provide for a small salary. I wanted to take eight conferences a year out to the Midwest states, have a weekly Bible study, deliver monthly meetings and I wanted revival for my rural area.

But I also added to that long list of requests. My heart's desire was to pray specifically that the building, wherever it was and whatever it looked like, could have a main entry and two large rooms. An entry way would say to the person, "Here we are!" One room would be used for meetings and one room would host a desk, kitchen, and bathroom. Nothing we had seen prior to this day offered what was on my prayer list.

As I drove up the rural Murdock country road to the little church, I could see it resting peacefully in the distance. The surrounding scenery was breathtaking. To my right, I saw Frank Lake, all still and blue-green, with a swan gliding along the center. Birds flittered about from tree to tree as though welcoming me. There was a strange feeling in my soul, as though time had passed and had somehow forgotten the beautiful little area. Although it felt deserted and abandoned, as I approached the driveway, I saw the lawn had been immaculately mowed.

A blackbird cawed out from a branch of a nearby tree. I looked at the deep blue of the sky and marveled at the lovely soft, billowy clouds that hovered over the church.

I remember thinking ... it looks small.

But it was old and anyone who knew me well ... knew

old buildings,

old people,

old stories,

& old songs

are my favorite things in life.

I apprehensively walked up to the big white doors. I noticed someone had tried to break in, as the door handle was bent and the wood was chipped.

Pressing hard, I was able to open the door, and step into the most glorious feeling.

It was as though time had stood still. For in these few moments, time greeted me and ushered me into 1900.

Gasping, I stood in the entry way, looked straight ahead into a large side room, and then stepped to the left entering a large sanctuary.

The old sacred building enveloped me. The musty smell comforted me. The idea of this building for our ministry intrigued me.

But one thing was for sure. I knew within the first moment of stepping beyond those doors … this was it! This church was the answer to my long-time prayers and I knew beyond a shadow of a doubt, the journey of a lifetime was just beginning.

❦ Buying The Church ❧

Your people will rebuild the ancient ruins and will raise up the age-old foundations;
You will be called repairer of broken walls, restorer of streets with dwellings.
Isaiah 58:12

In the last few months prior to seeing the little church for sale on the front page of the April 24, 2012, *West Central Tribune,* Willmar, Minnesota, I had diligently poured over my Bible. I hoped and prayed God would give me some sign, some comfort on what was to come.

There was scripture that continually popped up in my devotional time and stood out to me, as though the words danced off the page into air in front of me so that I would see them and know them. That scripture was Isaiah 58:12, but as I looked at the words, I was confused.

The scripture began, "Your people will *rebuild* the ancient ruins and will *raise up* the age-old foundations ..." But what did that mean? I thought it meant we'd purchase the little school building and repurpose the old walls and floors.

Next, it said, "You will be called *repairer* of broken walls, *restorer* of streets with dwellings." I thought it must mean that we would fix the things that were broken and that as people drove by on Highway 29, they'd say, "Wow, that building has been repurposed."

One week before I was standing in front of the little church, my friend Kathleen called me.

Kathleen served as Director of Prayer for Best Life Ministries. As she was praying for a building for headquarters, she came across the same scripture and called me. She said, "Write this passage down and look it up with Dean. God is prompting me that this passage is for you right now as you search for a building. I don't know what it means, but it is Isaiah 58:12."

I was dumbfounded that it was the same scripture, but I remembered learning as a child from my daddy, that when God continues to put the same thing in front of you, you must pay attention!

That morning of April 24, I never would have guessed that the meaning of the scripture and the reality that what it said was about to happen, would all be rolled up in one neat little package. The future of the church and our destiny were about to collide.

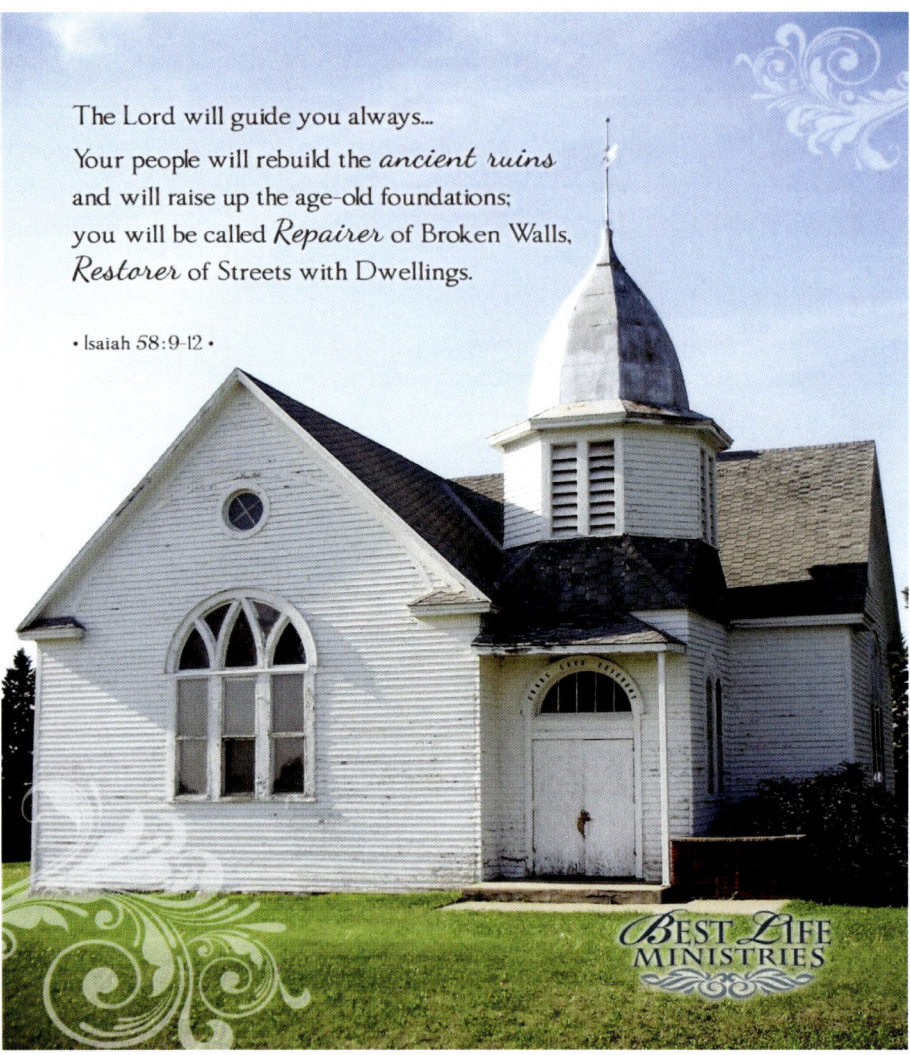

As I stood in the church entryway waiting to meet Dennis Johnson, the man selling the building, I looked around at the wood paneling and the old red tiled floor. I stepped into the sanctuary and took in the old light-oak pews, the cream-colored tin ceiling, the upright piano that sat on stage, the huge podium covered with blonde oak and the communion table in front of it.

Above everything else, hanging on the front wall of the church in place of any audacious carvings or ornate cross, hung Warner Sallman's beautiful picture of *Christ at Heart's Door*, which was painted in the late 1940s.

I noticed that the windows panes were made of a beautiful bubble glass in the royal colors of purple and yellow.

As I walked into the side room, it was almost half the size of the sanctuary and hosted a small corner for a kitchen, sporting a big electric stove left over from the 1950s.

I walked back to the sanctuary, sat in a back pew and closed my eyes to pray. In a flickering instant within my decorating brain, I saw the entire church. I saw it not as it was, but as how God intended it to be.

In my mind, I saw warm lighting coming from the antique fixtures. I saw beautiful soft curtains that hung from the top of the window to the bottom, on the two largest windows. I saw pictures hanging on the walls of the history of the church's past. I saw a small kitchen with sink, refrigerator, counter to serve coffee, table and chairs, rugs, and a desk. Lastly, I saw the old door that headed out back to the cemetery, but in its place, when the door opened, I pictured a bathroom.

I was awakened out of my prayer time by the shutting of the front door and I looked up to see a tall man, white hair and glasses, who seemed very kind and quiet. "I'm Dennis Johnson," he stated. "What do you think of the church?"

How could mere words tell this man of my past? How could I describe in a few sentences the years that had passed where I had asked God for my heart's desire and He had directed me right here? How could I possibly let this stranger know my deepest desire was to give him $1 and know that this would be headquarters for our ministry?

 ❧ Dennis & Marie Johnson ☙
Spearheaded the Sale
of the Frank Lake Covenant Church
for the Hillside Cemetery Association
(On the lawn at the Frank Lake Church)

In my excitement, I told him everything I loved about the building. I quickly raced through my sad story of my child being attacked and my ministry. I told him about my search for a building, how we couldn't afford anything we saw, and how our neighbors said to pray for an old church. Then, I told him how twelve hours later, we saw this on the front page.

Dennis nodded as he took everything in and said, "Well, there have been several others who are interested in the church." My heart sank. I wasn't getting anywhere.

He asked me, "What are your intentions for the building?"

And I began to unfold my God-vision for Bible studies, monthly and community-wide events and offices.

Dennis looked around the building and told me, "You know, my grandfather, father and uncle all helped start up this church. My family went here for many years. It will be so sad to see it go. I'll have to go home and discuss things with my wife Marie."

And just like that, I felt things slipping away. Uncertain how to convince this man that my heart that loved God and loved old things would treasure every moment of living life in the building, I said a quiet prayer in my heart and asked God for help.

The answer came swiftly as I heard the words roll off my tongue. "Mr. Johnson, I was a worship director for churches over the past twenty-five years. I started my career at Plymouth Covenant. This is an old Swedish Covenant church, right?" I asked.

He nodded as I continued. I looked around the sanctuary and said, "I know Swedish."

Dennis looked at me surprised and said, "Really?"

I walked right up to the old upright piano and lifted the cover from the keyboard. I began to gently press the ivory keys, marveling at the fact that the piano didn't seem out of tune for a 1920's piano that hadn't been played for thirty-two years. I started the introduction to "Tryggare Kan Ingen Vara" ("Children of the Heavenly Father") and began to quietly sing the first verse.

Dennis began to sing along with me and tears began to roll down his cheeks. While we sang that verse, I breathed a prayer of thanksgiving to Mrs. Margaret Johnson, my neighbor from Clarinda, Iowa, who took me in every week for gingersnaps and taught me hymns in Swedish.

When the song was finished, I asked, "Would you like your dollar now or later?"

Dennis smiled and said, "I'll go home now and talk with my wife. I'll call you."

The wonderful world of cellular phones helped me out as I dialed Dean and told him everything that had just taken place. My words tumbled out so quickly that Dean could hardly keep up with me.

"Mr. Johnson says we have to move the church off the property. That would mean that you'd have to give up some land, Dean," I said while cringing. I knew that farmers loved the same things in life. They loved God, their mamas, and the land. This would be a miracle for Dean to give up some of his land for this dream, and quite honestly, at that point in time, it was more my dream than his.

I remember how directly he answered me while he responded, "We'll see."

All of a sudden, I was back at my home church in Iowa and was four years old. I was sitting by my daddy on the pew, so close to him that I could hear his words whispered in my ear to this day. He said, "Kathleen, honey, you have to move over, you're too close to Daddy." I can't hold my Bible."

When I responded, "Can I sit by you on the way home, Daddy?"

He smiled so tenderly down at me and said, "We'll see."

My dad's famous words for my entire life ... we'll see.

It didn't mean yes, it didn't mean no. What it meant for me was that I was going to need to start praying. I'd need to pray for Mr. Johnson and his wife, and for my dear farmer to release some of his grove.

The interesting part that I knew about Dean's grove was this: nothing would grow there. We'd been married for seven years and I had watched him working on the grove. For years he'd planted bushes and shrubs, trees and flowers, but nothing would take hold.

I asked him often why nothing would grow there and he always said, "I just don't get it. I can't figure it out. There was an old house here that was torn down; maybe the soil just doesn't want to respond to plants."

I drove home and nervously paced the house, praying and thinking. About 2:00 p.m., LuElla Young called me to see if I had seen the little church on the front page of the newspaper.

After work that same day, Dean drove up with me to see the church. I watched his face as we drove up and I saw a light come across his eyes with a little glimmer of interest. It was a good sign!

Out came the tape measure and the farmer took notes as he measured this and that. I walked through the rooms again, thanking and praising the goodness of the God who had allowed this church to sit empty for thirty-two years, knowing that exactly when Kathy and Dean were looking for a building, God would release the hold on the building and allow it to be ready for sale. Once again I marveled at God's perfect timing.

We drove home and while I waited in the house, Dean went to measure the grove. He ran into the house with excitement and disbelief on his face. "I measured it, Ma'am, and exactly the size of the church, 40' x 36', is exactly the empty spot in the grove where nothing will grow! It's not meant to grow plants or trees. It's meant to grow a ministry!"

As we sat down in the kitchen, Dean grabbed his cold Mt. Dew and I sipped my iced tea and we began to seriously talk about what it meant to move a church. The more we talked, the more my husband became nervous and worried. The more we talked, the more I became confident that God was in the details and it would work out, but to appease my husband, I called Mr. Johnson.

I asked him to contact the Hillside Cemetery Association board and ask them if we could buy the church and keep it on the property it was on in rural Murdock, Minnesota, next to Frank Lake.

Dennis was apprehensive at the request, but assured me that he and his wife had discussed our potentially purchasing the church. I had the opportunity to talk with his wife, Marie, and loved her instantly. I knew in my heart that no matter what would happen, I wanted this couple to be our friends. They were marvelous.

Dennis promised to connect with the board while Dean and I waited, prayed, planned, and processed.

That night, we went to bed and I led the prayer for the closing of the day. I asked God to show us what to do, to reveal His plan, and to give that wisdom to the board and the Johnsons.

It was a fitful night's sleep. Dean tossed and turned and while he was tossing, I was praying. I put my hand on his shoulder and asked God to help him release his grove.

The next morning was bright and sunny. My husband looked at me and said, "I've made up my mind." I took a deep breath and released the future to God. Dean said, "We're moving the church here. I thought about it all night. The church must be here in the grove. That's final." I hugged and thanked him and thanked God.

A short while later the phone rang and Mr. Johnson informed me that the board discussed it and they felt that the church had to be moved to the grove. But you see how God worked in the matter? If they would have insisted that before my husband came to his own decision, it might not have worked out the way it did. God's timing was perfect.

We were instantly propelled forward on the journey and began some of the most wonderful days we have lived through thus far.

We met with Dennis and Marie and signed a contract to purchase Frank Lake Covenant Church for $1. We gave Dennis a crisp one dollar bill, hugged and thanked them, and drove to see the building that God had provided for Best Life Ministries and the Weckwerths.

As the two of us walked quietly into the church, we heard the songs of the birds in the trees around us. We saw the church not as it was, but as it would be, for I never saw the old rotting boards, chipped paint, or birds' feathers in the pews. No instead, I saw something of real beauty. It made me realize that this is how our Heavenly Father sees us. Not as the work that needs to be done, but as the work that will be done.

⤞ Dean Weckwerth ⤝
Seeing the Church for the First Time

Dean and I walked up to the altar. We knelt in front of the picture of Jesus and we folded our hands and we bowed our heads to pray. As I prayed, tears streamed down my face. I looked at my husband, I looked at my Savior's picture, and I realized the full meaning of the verse He had provided.

We would *raise* it up off of its old foundation.

We would *repair* the leaks in the roof and walls.

We would *rebuild* the broken windows and doors.

We would refurbish, repaint, and replace the broken boards.

And eventually, we would be known as the couple who *restored* a building and put it in their grove right next to Highway 29, south of Benson, Minnesota.

❦ Kathy Speaking at Frank Lake ❦

The Foundation

Consequently, you are no longer foreigners and strangers,
but fellow citizens with God's people and also members of His household,
built on the foundation of the apostles and prophets,
with Christ Jesus Himself as the chief cornerstone.
Ephesians 2:19-20

I remember during those weeks of preparing to move the church that a strong presence of the Holy Spirit rested on every call we made, every person we talked with, and every news reporter that connected with us. God was moving things forward and no human could stop His work.

Once the purchase contract was signed, Dean and I began to lay the plans for a new foundation in the grove. We made calls, chatted with family and friends, and got constructive advice. Much would need to be accomplished before the church would be lifted off of its old foundation from 1900, and moved twenty-six miles to our home south of Benson to be set upon its new the foundation.

The first thing we needed to do was to find a mover. We originally called a company in Willmar and then another by St. Cloud to get bids. But when Jim Thein from Thein Moving Company personally showed up at the church to give us a bid, there was something that completely clicked for us. Jim was kind and knowledgeable, and for two people who'd never moved a building, let alone been around anyone who had, we trusted his advice.

We found out that Thein Moving Company had been around since the late 1800s and had moved all kinds of buildings. Their family and crew were exceptional to work with, and from the moment we met Jim, we were in good hands.

A television show called *Massive Moves*, from the station HGTV out of Canada, contacted us and asked if we would allow them to follow us during the journey. Once we agreed, we received two more calls; one from PBS, Appleton, Minnesota, and one from *On the Road with Jason Davis* (KSTP/ABC), Minneapolis, Minnesota, asking if they could follow the move as well. We happily agreed!

Newspaper reporters from the *West Central Tribune*, Willmar, Minnesota, *Montevideo American-News*, Montevideo, Minnesota, and the Twin Cities called to interview us about the move. Editor Reed Anfinson of the *Swift County Monitor-News*, Benson, Minnesota, contacted me about going to see the church, and then coming to the grove and writing an article about our plans for the future of the ministry.

On the home front, we began to set up details for the movers: the electrical companies to move their lines, a tree-trimmer to cut trees that would hit the top of the church, a masonry crew to pour the foundation, electricians, plumbers, and carpenters.

As we look back at this time, we realize that God gave us the energy, the connections, and the finances to be able to move forward. Many of our neighbors, family members, friends, and staff, gave generously to help the move occur.

One of the calls we had to make was to the Swift County Planning and Zoning Administrator to acquire a building permit. They sent out a man who surveyed the grove and checked out the sewer system. Everything was fine until we mentioned we were moving a church.

Something happens to people when you use the word "church." Either happy worshipful connotations arise, or some great dark fear torments the soul. Whatever way this was headed, I knew it was time for prayer. After the gentleman left the grove, I took off my sandals and raised my hands to the heavens. I began to pray and worship.

The sun was shining brightly through the big silver poplars when I stepped out to where the church would reside. I looked up to the heavens and began to sing the song "I Stand in Awe" by Mark Altrogge.

> You are beautiful beyond description,
> too marvelous for words.
> Too wonderful for comprehension,
> like nothing ever seen or heard.
> Who can grasp Your infinite wisdom?
> Who can fathom the depths of Your love?
> You are beautiful beyond description,
> majesty enthroned above.
> And I stand, I stand in awe of You.
> I stand, I stand in awe of You.
> Holy God to whom all praise is due,
> I stand in awe of You.

We needed God to keep moving ahead and leading the way. We needed open doors and all of His goodness.

Later that afternoon the phone rang and everything was apprehensively approved.

Throughout the upcoming weeks, Dean worked hard to map out where the new bathroom would be located and where the foundation would be poured.

Psalm 34:9 was on my mind during those weeks:

Worship God if you want the best;
Worship opens doors to all His goodness.

❧ Kathy & Dean Weckwerth ☙
Stand in the Grove that Would Ultimately Host the Church

Caren Hanson of Hanson Concrete had done work for us before. He drove up to the church to review and then back to our grove to get an idea of where the church would sit.

I remember the day that he drove to Frank Lake Covenant, still at its original location, to check things out. My dear friend, Mary Anderstrom, was visiting the church with me that afternoon.

Mary was an important part of the journey for me personally. The first day I arrived at my church job in Willmar, Mary supported me. From that moment on, we became fast friends.

One day Mary came into my office after the ministry had been birthed. She agreed to become my Director of Prayer and Care Support. I didn't fully grasp the goodness of God at the time because it never really sunk into my heart and brain how important Mary's friendship really was.

Mary had served as the Women's Ministry Director for the General Baptist Conference for the state of Minnesota for many years. What I didn't understand at the time was that Mary would be influential with her knowledge of women's ministry in helping me to understand further what I needed to know to create a valuable, effective ministry.

All I had ever done, since I was twelve years old, was plan services and deliver music in churches. I didn't know a thing about women's ministry ... but Mary did.

On that day that she came into my office, she brought two freshly-made caramel rolls in a little basket with a beautiful cloth napkin covering them. A fork, knife, and two small pats of butter were inside the basket. She placed on my desk alongside the caramel rolls, an icy-cold glass of tea with a lemon wedge. She smiled and said, "Kathy, my dear, I want to talk with you about something."

❧ Mary Anderstrom ☙
Supporter, Encourager, Prayer Warrior

I had been so busy that day, but I always made time for Mary. She sat down on my couch in the office while I munched on delicate bites of sugary goodness. She began by saying, "You know that I love you and believe in you like you were my own, right?"

I smiled and nodded.

"I want you to hear me, really hear me, when I tell you this. Someday you will not be sitting here. Someday you will be working full time at this ministry, Best Life, and God will use you to help so many more, and reach so many more than you are doing right now."

I cringed. Leave my beloved job? How could she say this? I remember rebuffing her and saying, "No! I couldn't ever stop being a worship director."

Her kind, wise eyes were hurt for a moment and then she looked at me, past my ignorance and my age and said, "Okay, honey. It's okay. God will do what He needs to when the time comes. But for now, just think and pray about it."

I agreed to do that, but felt so scared.

Three years later, my friends Kathleen and Mary were with me at Mary's home by Diamond Lake outside of Willmar, Minnesota. It was a day filled with mixed emotions as I was leaving my church to go full time with Best Life Ministries. I remember crying and it was more than past due what I said to Mary. I said, "You were so right. I am going full time and I won't be a worship director anymore."

Mary answered me with, "You'll go further now and do more for God. Just wait and see what's in store for you and Dean."

It wasn't much longer when Mary's cancer returned. She had battled it successfully, but this time it came back with a vengeance. As I listened to her doctor while Mary lay in the hospital bed, we both wept as we heard the news. Mary made the decision not to fight anymore, but to give in and allow her journey to finally take her to the throne of God.

But Mary never wanted to give up on me and my dreams. In her final days, as frail and sweet as she was, she asked if I would pick her up and take her to Murdock to see the church. I happily agreed and we went to see the church. Mary was elated with everything about the little church. She said she could see it restored and at our property.

That day, Mary sat in the front pew of the church. We called her sister, Maxine, on my cell phone and we prayed together and blessed the church. We also sang "How Great Thou Art" and "How Great is Our God" together. Knowing that this would be the one and only time my dear friend would see her prophetic dream about me and the ministry coming true, we sat and rested in the pews while the afternoon drifted by.

That's when Caren Hanson came to the church to visit. My sweet friend, Mary, listened as Caren talked about a family member who had cancer. Listening, nodding, comforting, and never ever mentioning that she was walking through her final days with cancer, she emulated the heart of Christ. She cared and loved with all focus on someone other than herself.

Mary and I talked that day about the foundations of Best Life Ministries. She told me that God would never honor pride from leaders. That every single woman at an event mattered, and that I was a leader who should always take my directives from God and never from humans.

Mary reminded me that the solid foundation of any relationship, whether marriage, friendship, family, or ministry, would have to be Jesus Christ. And she always said that the next stone layered upon that foundation must be prayer.

We left the little church that day, a little more somber, a little more realistic, and a lot more relieved that together we had seen the day that her vision was taking life.

I am reminded of an excerpt of Mary's journal after she found out about her cancer returning:

> *Remembering not to forget the wonderful times and then trying to forget the hard times is what develops in the midst of life.*
>
> *There's a certain inborn desire that prompts me to prepare for and to pursue life. In my seventy-seven years of life, you may assume I've learned how to prepare and to pursue life with a purpose.*
>
> *You may assume I know what it's like to set goals expecting to achieve them. And what you may also assume is that when my assumptions are altered by unexpected interruptions I wonder what in the world the purpose is. Lest I forget, it's remembering not to forget that God prepares me for the expected and the unexpected realities in life.*

This was 'unexpected realities.'

Cancer would take my friend, but she would see the reality of her vision beginning to unfold before she left this earth.

Back at the grove, Dean had cleared some small old brush. Caren Hanson and his crew had mapped out and poured the concrete that created a firm foundation for the little church. Just like that, the grove changed. Instead of there being huge old trees that surrounded an empty center, there were now huge old trees that were surrounding a newly laid foundation. Where nothing would grow, a church was being planted.

The bathroom addition was included in the plan. Dennis Johnson had told us we could move the outhouses, should we choose. We chose to leave them behind.

In all of those moments waiting for carpenters and building permits, watching for cement mixers and crews, I could hardly wait for the day when the old building would sit on its new foundation.

And through it all, I continually reminded myself and Dean that our lives, our hopes and dreams, were all planted firmly on the foundation of God Almighty, Father of Abraham, Isaac and Jacob. We would remember Mary's words of encouragement and Ephesians 2:19-20.

The church would be built *on the foundation of God, the apostles and prophets*—on the foundation of faith, hope and prayer—

Jesus Christ would be the cornerstone.

~ The Route ~

*And I'll stride freely through wide open spaces
as I look for Your truth and wisdom.
Psalm 119:45*

When it came time to sit down to map out the route for the church move, an old fashioned road map was used. Jim Thein from Thein Moving Company and Dean would map the route from Frank Lake to our grove.

We climbed up in Jim's old red truck and headed out to the church. Along the way, Jim told us stories of the surrounding territory, of old houses and churches, and of some of the experiences they had while moving buildings.

Time flew by quickly until we arrived at the church. Each time I saw it, I felt like a piece of my heart was reconnected. It felt like the church was waiting for us and we were waiting for it.

We started at the church and drove several different country roads that would lead us right back to our property.

The drive was lovely and all I saw were trees, old farmhouses and fields of grain.

Dean and Jim, on the other hand, saw bridges, bumps, curves and tree branches.

As they plotted and planned, I imagined the day's arrival for the big move. The church would be driven down old country roads in wide open spaces.

Once we got back to the grove, Jim recommended a kind man named Al who would help us take down the old decrepit chimney at the church before the move. Al would also trim tree branches along the route that would be too low for the height of the church while it was being moved.

My job was to travel with Dean to each farmer's home along the planned route. We intended to knock on their doors, introduce ourselves and explain the upcoming church move. The goal was to get their permission to trim any branches that were hanging over the road that were too low.

Although the job sounded daunting, it ended up being fulfilling. Many of the neighbors of the old church thanked us and told us how much they appreciated what we were doing in saving the church and moving it to another location.

They were pleased that the old church, built by the faithful with pennies, nickels and dimes, would continue to serve the area and community through Best Life Ministries.

The church was small but large when moved down roads, over railroad tracks, and under power lines. The route plan was in place, the neighbors contacted, and trees trimmed. Thein Moving Company acquired the road permits, as well as the permit to cross the railroad tracks.

We contacted three different electrical companies about power lines that were too low for the church to pass under. The men from the electrical companies worked diligently to make the route clean and easy. They found the shortest distances that would have only a few electrical lines in the way of the church.

Since I married Dean and moved out to the country, I have complained about the wide open spaces of nothingness. Everywhere I looked there were fields. I wanted buildings and Targets, children playing and Walmarts, the sound of lawn mowers and a nearby Panera Bread.

Instead, I have the swish of tree branches blowing in the wind, the occasional sound of a cow that needs milking, a lonely coyote's cry, or the house wren's chirp.

I have thought over and over again that if I had been living in a town or city, this would have been impossible.

ROUTE FOR CHURCH MOVE	MILES
Church Begins @ 1280 20th St. NE	
From Church go west on 20th St. NE	0.6
Turn left on MN Hwy. 9	0.1
Turn left on Co. Rd. 33	3.0
Turn right on 30th St. SE	7.0
Turn left on 50th Ave. SE	3.0
Turn left on 60th St. SE	0.5
Turn right on 50th Ave. SE	6.0
Turn right on 120th St. SE	4.0
Turn right on MN Hwy. 29	1.7
Turn right off MN Hwy. 29	0.1
New Location @ 1025 Hwy. 29 SE	
Total Miles	**26.0**

I would never have been able to house a large old church on my property in the city with Panera Bread sitting next to it. Instead, God knew all along that my path, with all of its curves and twists, would end up on a straight and narrow road called Highway 29 in the middle of nowhere.

Dean and I looked at the path set out for the church move. It was wide open with fields on either side. The church would be moved down country roads on Tuesday, August 14, 2012, and my heart would meet the desires of God's heart … a headquarters … a home for Best Life Ministries.

I looked out in the distance and said to Dean, "This is the road that the church will come down." His gaze was far away and distant as he nodded.

Then I quietly whispered to him and to God, "And this is the blessing of living in the middle of nowhere … *in wide open spaces.*"

∽ Summer 2015 ∾

~ The Cleaning ~

*Then I will sprinkle clean water on you,
and you will be clean;*
Ezekiel 36:25a

Excitement had been rising within the Weckwerth household, and Dean and I were working diligently to prepare for the upcoming transition between the church being in rural Murdock for 112 years, and the church moving to our farm.

With our full-time jobs and all the extra requirements of planning, scheduling, and preparing, life was being driven by huge amounts of prayer, caffeine, and adrenalin.

The HGTV crew was coming from England. They would be flying into the Twin Cities and then driving to Benson to stay for three weeks. They wanted us to know they would be following our every move. We were not well-versed in the art of acting, so that brought great distress to my shy, quiet farmer-husband.

Dennis and Marie would check in with us daily. We would pray with them and share the never-ending details that were filled with excitement as we prepared for the move.

One day before the television crew arrived, Marie called me and said she thought it would be a good idea to give the church a good cleaning before it transferred owners. She had called and arranged for several of the old members and their families to meet at the church and spend some time cleaning it, in order to prepare for the upcoming going away service that we were planning. I thought it was a marvelous idea!

Although I had no idea what to expect, I knew whatever they did, I wanted to be with them. I wanted to meet these people, thank them for their generosity, and find out all I could about the church's past. I also knew it would be a challenging time together since the little church had no electricity or running water.

From the pages of my journal, I share this excerpt of my experience from the day of the church cleaning:

The day had been a scorcher, but now there were big drops of rain splashing against my windshield. I looked out at the fields around me, and focused my thoughts on what it must have been like to live out here, in this countryside, and wait for Sunday morning church. What was it like for those people in 1898, who prepared for the morning service by getting their wagons hitched up and their horses ready to go?

I smiled as I drove the familiar gravel road, the rain stopping as abruptly as it started. The lake was to my right and the hill with the church to my left. I stopped for a moment and looked at the lake. I could almost hear the voices from the past singing, "Holy, Holy, Holy! Lord God Almighty! God in three persons, Blessed Trinity!" as I continued to drive and put the car in park.

It was an amazing sight. There were at least seven or eight cars parked there at the little church and people were unloading mops, brooms, dustpans, and vacuum cleaners. A kind little grandpa was unloading a generator and shook my hand asking, "Are you related to the Weckwerth wrestlers from Benson?"

"Yes," I smiled as I replied.

I unloaded my cleaning supplies and took a deep breath. I knew only two of these people. They were the kind couple that sold me the church, Dennis and Marie Johnson.

Dennis, always gentle in spirit and conscientious about everything, was carefully removing the storm windows from the church. While Marie, always bright and bubbly, was asking me to take charge and organize the troops.

We opened in a word of prayer, and set off to scrub, sweep and dust. The heat of the day was overwhelming until we felt a cool breeze coming through. I looked up. I looked past the vacuum, past the pile of debris and past the laughing voices as they reminisced over the past and stories of their childhood, and I listened. I listened for the Spirit of God and His voice. I responded to that prompting, that voice that reminded me to be so very thankful. I stopped for a moment and breathed a silent prayer of thanks and gratitude.

It isn't everyday that someone gets to buy a church. It isn't everyday that a ministry gets to utilize the building and carry on the mandate of worship from God. And in today's world, it isn't everyday that you get to watch strangers come together and say, "I'll help you clean your church."

We finished up quickly. I remembered my grandmother's famous line, "Many hands make light work." Then I headed outside to dump some dirty water, where I heard the men chatting excitedly about the goodbye service that would take place right there on Sunday, July 29, 2012, at 2:00 p.m.

I walked with Marie out to the gravestones and reviewed several of the names. It seemed as though so many of the dates revealed that many of the congregants had died so very young.

I wondered how they were a part of the history of the life of this church.

Today, I am thankful.

Today I am reminded that when people join

Together for a common cause for good, we are community.

We are doing the very thing God wants us to do ...

"Love one another as you love yourself" (Mark 12:31a).

To those dear souls who helped clean this week, I am so very thankful.

We were ready for Sunday!

That day was so very special to me. Simplistic in every way—the old mops, the brooms, the carrying in of buckets and jugs of water, and the homey smell of lemon overtook the old musty vapors. The friends and neighbors who joked and reminisced made me feel so comfortable.

Although there was a small amount of sadness that one would naturally feel after loving something for so long, the people were grateful the building would not continue to fall into disrepair, or worse yet, be burned down.

The cleaning was completed that day and shortly after, the television crews and reporters would arrive to begin following the journey. God was working and we were waiting. It wouldn't be long until we saw the church journey really begin to move forward. Everything was made right again, washed anew—washed *clean*.

❧ Many Hands Make Light Work ☙

❧ The Goodbye Service ❦

*Therefore, if anyone is in Christ,
the new creation has come:
The old has gone, the new is here!
II Corinthians 5:17*

We had successfully purchased the church, found the mover, planned the route, cleaned the building and the move was scheduled on the calendar. However, I felt like something was missing.

The church had been sitting empty for thirty-two years and I felt the people from the original congregation, the neighbors and friends, and the old church building itself, needed a proper goodbye.

I called and discussed with Dennis and Marie Johnson how we could approach planning a service that would include a grateful send-off and a thankful welcome all wrapped into one big package.

We quickly arranged matters by contacting old church members and families, advertising in the *Swift County Monitor-News*, Benson, and the *Kerkhoven Banner* newspapers, and publicizing on social media. Our Best Life Ministries' staff videographer created a short advertisement with me at the church as I talked about the building, the blessings, and the upcoming service.

By then the *West Central Tribune*, *Kerkhoven Banner*, and the *Swift County Monitor-News* newspapers were alerted. The Appleton PBS television station, as well as the HGTV crew, would arrive to cover and record the service.

Dennis and Marie contacted the only surviving pastor, Pastor Richard Lundgren from Turner, Oregon. Pastor Lundgren had served Frank Lake Covenant from 1953-1959 and was excited about returning for the event.

I cannot explain the energy that was electric running through the conversations, letters, emails and phone calls. Everywhere Dean and I looked, we saw God at work through others. The original Swedish choir members were contacted and asked to sing. I couldn't believe that the same beautiful voices that were on the record I purchased on eBay would now be standing in front of me and others, singing the cherished Swedish hymns from so long ago.

The church had been cleaned and women from the Murdock and Kerkhoven area had prepared the lunch that would be served at the goodbye service. With no electricity or running water, the service would be as it was in the early 1900s.

July 29, 2012, was cool and that in itself was an answer to prayer. The sun was bright in the beautiful deep-blue sky that hosted big puffy clouds swirling about like whipped cream.

I craned my neck out the church window to take one last look at where the church had stood these past 112 years. I knew we would shortly experience its last service in the location by its nearby friend that sat across the road, the actual lake named, Frank Lake.

Dennis and Marie Johnson had worked diligently to get things ready. I was relieved for them and thankful that their kind children and grandchildren had rallied around them to help with hard work and generous support.

As I entered the church that morning, I took a deep breath and said, "God, let this day be honoring to You. Let it be a celebration of the past and an anticipation of the future. But mostly, let it all be about you."

Dean carried in boxes and tables, while the HGTV film man followed us around, ever so calmly continuing to be in the way. I nervously set up the easels with the old pictures that Wendall Falk and several of Dennis' family had shared. I had enlarged and framed the photos in big black frames. As I gently set them on each easel and arranged some burlap around the tops, I looked at them and felt a strong connection with the people who once stood in that same spot, probably getting ready for a service to begin, just like I was.

There was a heaviness that I felt. I couldn't quite pin it down, but I continued to set out big pots of ivy and ferns and arranged them on the altar.

As the tables were being set up, I prepared the ice tea pot and glasses, and set out the boxes of ginger snaps and sugar cookies that I had baked.

The red checkered table cloths were set to go, and I looked up to see Dennis and Marie walking in with an air of vigor and enthusiasm.

A sweet dear soul named Dick Carlson came in and spoke softly. "Right here, Kathy," he said. "Right here is where Dennis and I stood and we looked at each other and said, 'It will have to be torn down,'" and then his voice choked up and tears gathered in the corner of his eyes.

He could no longer speak, and so I added "But it isn't going to have to be torn down or burned, is it! Thank God for how He works in such wonderful ways!"

I hugged him and felt blessed that God had stirred in the hearts of these two dear souls that it was time to do something about the building. When we are in the eleventh hour, God comes in to the rescue. God partnered a little girl from Southwest Iowa, who had hopes and dreams to house a ministry (and deepest dreams to have it be in an old building, let alone an old church, joy unspeakable!) with some hearts that treasured their sweet building and what God had accomplished throughout history inside those walls. Oh, what a fabulous God that we have!

I looked down at my watch and surveyed the room. I took a deep breath and glanced over my music as people started coming in the sanctuary. It was early!

The kind folks that made up the Swedish choir were trickling in to prepare for their rehearsal. But I was taken aback by a wonderful woman who came up and took my arm and looked deeply into my eyes.

This stranger said words of comfort to me that I will never forget. She said, "Kathy, if anyone anywhere does not believe that this is God's will and that God orchestrated all of this, then they just don't know God."

And just like that ... she walked away. My eyes were filled with tears and I knew then what the nagging feeling inside was that I couldn't put my finger on until that moment. I felt a responsibility. I felt an overwhelming burden that today would not only bring honor to God, but I knew that I needed to make this service as enjoyable, as comforting, and as promising for those in attendance as I possibly could.

As a Director of Worship and Creative Arts for many years, I have planned so many services that my family teases me that I could plan and deliver services in my sleep. Most of those services have been connected with a high level of responsibility. This service, this one would be included with the many others that I felt so strongly about.

Crowds of people began to arrive while many older folks brought memorabilia of days gone by. There were people from Rochester, Duluth, the Twin Cities and the surrounding rural towns. They were sharing photos and conversing over their pasts. Marie spread the memorabilia out on a table for people to look over, while Dennis and the men made sure that a large outdoor tent was secured and people were comfortable.

An overwhelming sense of comfort came over me, a strange peace of sorts, as I said hello to Pastor Lundgren. He was kind and funny, and when he spoke, you couldn't help but laugh. He was spreading such great cheer with his jokes and hearty laughter.

As the service began, with many people there and much media flittering about, I looked around the congregation and whispered to God, "Just think, long ago this would have been a normal Sunday service." And then the event began.

Dennis Johnson shared some details of the church, along with the dear grandpa, Dick Carlson, and then Pastor Richard Lundgren shared memories of his past service at the church. Inside jokes were laughed at, even if we didn't understand them completely, and the Swedish choir took its place.

The music filled the room and was superb worship that transcended above language. We could hear the melodious sounds, feel the emotions, and share in the flooding rush of the Holy Spirit, who dwells within the praise. Indescribable comfort and joy was what we felt as the deep rich harmonies of the group echoed throughout the building.

I had asked Best Life's worship leader and our good friend, Dave Herring, to lead several old hymns for the congregation to sing. Our good friend, Pastor Lewie Schultz, spoke as a representative for Best Life Ministries and blessed the past and promoted the future.

When I took my spot to close with the song "Praise the King," my voice cracked a few times at first. Normally, as a vocalist, I would have cringed. But not today! Today, I was fighting back emotion and tears. I knew that to sing those words and to allow my heart to fill the room with how I felt, would equate in tears being held back.

> *Praise Him in the morning*
> *For tall and lofty trees*
> *And praise Him in the evening*
> *For children on their knees*
> *Oh and praise Him in the noon day*
> *For gentle birds that sing*
> *Oh praise Him all ye people*
> *Praise the King*
> *Praise the King, Praise the King*
> *Let it ring, Praise the King*

My Nashville friend who is a worship artist, Cindy Morgan, wrote that song and it seemed quite fitting for the occasion. As the congregation joined in with me on the chorus, I felt such gratefulness, such relief, and such amazing love for God.

To think that God, in His infinite wisdom, would allow Frank Lake Covenant Church to partner with me was incredible. Here was a building rich in history of music and revival, partnered up with my heart, which is rich in history of music and revival. To try to understand how He worked out all the details, orchestrated the timing, and put everything together, was something I couldn't quite grasp.

That day, I was especially thankful to Dennis and Marie, dear Pastor Lundgren and the Swedish Choir, the sweet neighbors who prayed and prodded, Dick Carlson, and for Eric Carlson who thought to put it on Craigslist.

I was also grateful to Reed Anfinson from the *Swift County Monitor-News* and reporters from the *West Central Tribune* who covered our story, the HGTV crew who recorded it, and for the encouraging words of strangers who I never knew and may never meet again.

Many of our friends, family and staff came to support us, and the support meant everything to me.

I looked out at the crowd. The church was completely full with approximately 125 people. I was so thankful for all of those dear souls who came to the goodbye service to one last time cherish and relive the life that took place inside those walls.

The service ended with joyful hearts and mixed emotions. They hugged one last time. They glanced over their shoulders as they drove away. The church would not be there the next time they'd drive by on the country road.

Everything that once was would now be changed and different. Everything old would be made new.

But above and beyond to all of those fabulous people who made up the church from 1884-2012, I say this, "To the God of Abraham, Isaac and Jacob, who sent His son Jesus Christ to die for our sins, who loves us like no one else, and who put a vision in our hearts for the lost and the hurt …to You, God, *we thank You*."

*M*ay Frank Lake Covenant Church continue to house worship and service to You alone,
our *God who makes everything new* in His sight.

Friends Gather
July 9, 2012

 Swedish Choir

❧ Goodbye Service Scripture Reading ❧
Psalm 145:17

I will exalt You, my God the King;
I will praise Your name forever and ever.

Every day I will praise You
and extol Your name forever and ever.

Great is the Lord and most worthy of praise;
His greatness no one can fathom.

One generation commends Your works to another;
they tell of Your mighty acts.

They speak of the glorious splendor of Your majesty—
and I will meditate on Your wonderful works.

They tell of the power of Your awesome works—
and I will proclaim Your great deeds.

They celebrate Your abundant goodness
and joyfully sing of Your righteousness.

❧ Blue Skies & Farewell Blues ❧

The Preparation

*Prepare the way for the Lord,
make straight paths for Him.
Mark 1:3b*

Underneath the Church:

I had no idea what kind of work would be involved in the preparation of moving an old building, but I knew that the Theins were very experienced. Matt, Tim, and Jim Thein continually responded to our questions and concerns and gave us great comfort and hope that the move would be easy and smooth.

HGTV producer, Will Aspinall, and film tech, Rob Silver, set up at the church and filmed our every move. We adjusted into the mode of watching the Theins get the church readied for the move.

Morning sunrises and evening sunsets were taped by the film crew over and around the church.

For several days, Dennis, Marie and I would take our lawn chairs to the church and set them up under the big shady trees to watch the progress. An occasional robin would tweet out a song, while every once in a while, a bat would zip out of the bell tower.

A couple of those mornings, I would tell Dean I felt too tired to go sit in the sun and watch them prepare the church for the move. Dean would always say the same thing, "Ma'am, you won't see this more than once in this lifetime! You better get up there."

Matt and Tim Thein's first step to prepare the church was to jack it up. Once the sides were jacked up, they worked meticulously underneath the building to make sure the floor joists were strong enough to sustain the move. Cutting away old broken boards and replacing them with new sturdy ones, the time ticked by.

I remember that day when we first saw the church's firm foundation. I wasn't sure what to expect. I did not realize that once the corners of the building were lifted, we would see the huge field stones that were underneath the church.

Matt stopped and commented, "Did you see these huge stones? The farmers would dig them out and then men would use horses to drag them here and situate them to create a foundation. Can you imagine how heavy these are and how much work it would be to move them?"

I was quiet as I thought about the endless efforts this congregation had gone to in the fall of 1900, to

make sure that they were starting over with a sturdy foundation.

On one of the days that we watched, the television crew interviewed us about how we were feeling. I was elated. The Johnsons were happy that the church was going to good use, but they still felt an angst seeing the sweet little building prepare for its next step.

∂

Thein Moving Company Crew

∂

Removing the Steeple:

Once the joists underneath the church had been stabilized, the moving crew worked on the next big project ... removing the steeple.

According to road regulations, the church would be too tall to move with the steeple attached. It would need to be removed and would be pulled on a separate trailer behind the church.

I remember the day like it was yesterday. A huge crane was brought in to remove the steeple. Matt Thein was inside the lift that would help him to hook everything onto the steeple. The next thing I knew, Matt was asking if we had wasp spray. Dennis and Marie retrieved some from their nearby home and Matt was once again able to work.

Until we heard him say, "Kathy, I see little eyes and I don't like that!" Bats in the belfry! As the steeple was lifted, a couple of bats flew out past Matt. I remember screaming!

It took the morning and most of the afternoon for the steeple to be removed.

Journal Entry:

> *It was a strange feeling driving up to the church knowing that things would never be the same. Since the late 1800s, Frank Lake Covenant Church held a story. It held a story of music and worship, of love and community, of creativity, ingenuity, and salvation. The lives that have entered this building have been changed forever; that rings out so true in my heart every time I look at the white siding and the steeple.*

Today, the steeple is sitting on a truck and the church looks like it feels uncomfortable. I know, I know, I am a believer that we don't buy into inanimate objects having emotions, but the little church looked so forlorn today, so sad, and almost afraid.

The television crews were arriving and I was telling myself I would only stay for a short while. Again, another day of experiences that were so extraordinary, so odd for the every day-in-day-out life I live. I sighed a big sigh of relief as my friends, Dennis and Marie Johnson, pulled up. I felt so alone without Dean and the comfort of these friends made me feel better.

Thein movers pulled in shortly afterwards and we began the amazing watch as Frank Lake Covenant Church was lifted from its own old foundation and set upon dollies that were connected to a giant truck. But, I'm ahead of myself.

The morning began with a huge truck with long arms that went in underneath the church and attacked the large stones that made up the "ancient foundations." It would lift them high and they would smash to the ground as the driver continued. I cringed. There, in front of me were the ancient stones of yesteryears and they were smashing and crashing in front of my eyes. But I sat frozen in awe as he continued to dig the rocks out, quickly, effortlessly and release them into a large dirt/rock pile.

This continued for several hours as we visited, watched for bats and wasps, and walked around surveying the changes being made right in front of us.

I ran my hand over a large smooth stone, as I overheard someone say that the stones had been brought in from surrounding fields, and I closed my eyes, dreaming of the men who worked hard to create the foundation. I took a moment, bowed my head and thanked God for those dear souls.

Marie said that it was sad, but she knew that the church would be getting a new foundation now, and that brought her comfort.

❧ Dennis & Marie Johnson ☙
At the Original Site

Dennis Johnson
Reflecting on the Move Preparation

There was one moment in time where I was especially moved. Dennis stood in front of the church and just stood still looking, as though he could see something we couldn't. Perhaps a glimpse into his past attached to this wonderful building.

He told me his father, uncle, grandfather and great-uncle all attended here. His life was once a piece of life of that church and those stones being tossed to the side of the building now represented those lives.

I snapped a picture. And I thanked God that Dennis had been so kind as to go home and get me a couple of batteries for the continually used digital camera I clutched next to me.

Once the stones were dug out, quite a bit of dirt was dug out as well. We watched the men maneuver the equipment with expertise. And I thought how they were so skilled to do this job.

After the stones and dirt were moved, in came huge pieces of lumber to steady everything and I watched them knock out huge chunks of rock and stone. The very foundation that the church stood upon was being demolished.

Once the beams were in place, they brought in dollies and set them under the church. The dollies connected to a huge truck and I thought how I wished Dean was done with his shift delivering the mail and could watch with me.

I stood by myself in front of the church, watching as some fabulous machine made the very building raise in front of my eyes, ever so slowly. The rocks were falling from the bottom of the church and smashing in front of me and I looked up at the sky and quoted God's Word that He gave to us,

"*Your people will rebuild the ancient ruins and will raise up the age-old foundations.*"

The HGTV cameraman said, "What?" in his British accent. I answered, "It's the verse that God gave me. We will raise up the age old foundations and it's happening now. It's coming true and the foundation is being raised up in front of my eyes.

After awhile, as we continued to watch the move from under the trees, and had a little lunch of bologna sandwiches, cookies, and hot coffee poured from a thermos. It was a monumental time for all of us.

As Theins got everything prepared to drive the church out of the place it has called home for over 100 years, Dean walked up, just in time!

We watched hand-in-hand as the church was pulled to the end of the driveway.

The sky had cleared, the beautiful blue that I have learned to appreciate, along with some lovely puffy clouds that were above the rooftop, and I watched three small birds flit in a circle, making me think of Father, Son and Holy Ghost.

God has been so good to all of us. From the hearts' cry of men who didn't want to see the building burned down, to the prayers of our hearts as we searched for the next step for our ministry.

Today I await the next step ...

The biggest one of all.

The church comes to live here in the grove.

And I look up ever so high into the sky and realize,

It's just the beginning God, for us ...

The little church ...

And our future.

Thanks be to God for all He has done, is doing, and will do.

ಎ

The Church Lifted Off its Foundation

ಎ

ಎ

Kathy Takes Directions

ಎ

Preparation Complete:

The building's preparation was completed and now we awaited the actual move of the little church.

The church was on a trailer bed and the steeple was on a flatbed behind it.

Everything was prepared for the twenty-six mile trip to a new home.

❧ Ready to Roll ☙

❧

Dean Weckwerth
Arrives with a Smile

☙

Within the hours and moments that made up those days of preparation, Dean and I were busy working to get all the details in place. It was in the busyness that we became completely aware that the burden was on our shoulders to repurpose an old building. We weren't taking the responsibility lightly.

We knew that not only must we prepare the building, prepare the route, but we needed to prepare our hearts and minds for the undertaking.

In some of those moments, we each felt overwhelmed, but in those times, we were reminded of scripture and of God's faithfulness.

We firmly believed that God was in every detail of the preparation,

Because God doesn't call us to what we can do,

He calls us to what He can do.

The Neighbors

Greater love has no one than this:
to lay down one's life for one's friends.
John 15:13

Throughout the entire journey, God surrounded us with good friends.

Some days the friends would be there to meet us, greet us, help us and then go on their way. Other days, it was old friends who were in our lives for good or new friends who were staying around.

Whatever the friendship looked like, whether it was Mary Anderstrom, Kathleen and Jim Sogge, or Dennis and Marie Johnson, or our neighbors, Donald and LuElla Young, Walter and Mona Young, Vernie and Mona Bangsund, we were truly blessed with their friendship.

During all of the busyness, we needed a moment to catch our breath and decided to host a small picnic for the key players in our storyline. I made the calls, invited the friends, and relished in the fact that for one night, no one would be interviewing us, recording us, or asking us questions.

The gazebo sported fresh flowers and ferns and the grill was fired up. The tables were ready for dinner with our dear friends and neighbors. We looked forward to sitting down with those who had prayed for us, encouraged us, and believed in us.

The following is an excerpt from my journal of that evening:

I pulled Grandma's pitcher down from the cupboard. She once told me that she had used it when my dad was a little boy. It had six lovely glasses that go with the set, but I'm always too scared to use those. Today, I just fill the pitcher to the top with ice water, watching the lemon slices swirl to the top.

The day is horribly hot, and I worry that it will be too warm for our company to sit outside and enjoy our little backyard area. Dean has lit tiki torches and every outdoor lamp, washed the glass table tops and attached the umbrellas, and beautifully manicured the lawn.

I reach in our fridge for the cold potato salad I made with Bud and Marion's (Dean's parents) fresh baby red potatoes, and I pull out the dill pickles, quickly grabbing the brats and burgers to head to the grill. The Lays potato chips are looking very tempting as I pass by the big blue bowl and grab one, savoring the salty bite on my tongue.

The aroma of fresh brewed tea is flooding the air and I have attempted to create Dean's famous banana punch. Good grief, I don't know how he does it ... but I tried.

I take a deep breath and look around. Everything is ready for our company. Everything has been carefully prepared, so that we can put aside moments in time and thank these wonderful friends and neighbors, for their part in this journey ... the journey of the move of Frank Lake Covenant Church.

I hear a knock at the door and the evening begins. Laughter, hugs and excitement, electrify the rooms. Frank Sinatra and Dean Martin's voices are singing old love ballads from the 40s and I feel a calming peace as I look around the room.

While Dean is tending the grill, I get everyone seated. Here they are, these fabulous nine individuals who are making up the moments of time in our lives, and I pour our glasses of banana punch.

"I'd like to propose a toast," I say with my glass raised. The smiles and giggles reach my ears as I continue, "To each one of you who have played a part in this story. To LuVerne, who said 'no' to the schoolhouse and suggested, 'How about looking for an old church.'

"Here's to Mona and LuElla Young and JaVonne Frentzel who prayed with me to find the right place, and encouraged me over cups of coffee and tender prayers. To the other Mona, who prayed with Dean, LuVerne and me that afternoon, months ago. To Donald who called and said, 'What about an old church? Drive down and look at that old church and see what you think.'"

And then, I stood next to Dennis Johnson and put my hand on his shoulder and said, "And to Dennis and Marie, thank you for selling me your church for $1. Here's to everyone and how God uses all different people and pieces for His honor and glory." We clanked our plastic cups together and Dennis brushed his eyes, while I choked back my emotions.

I prayed and then we moved into enjoying the evening, our dinner, and one another's company.

We chatted about life. About cars and cats, about jobs and churches, and about one old church in particular. We laughed and swatted the bugs, and breathed in the fresh night air.

After we served up hot cups of coffee and red velvet cake with cream cheese frosting, we headed over to the grove to see where the church will go. It was the most important part of the evening, aside from thanking everyone for listening to God and being involved in a neighbor's hopes and dreams.

Dean and I led the guests to the bare spot in the center of the grove. "It will go right here," Dean said. Marie and I laughed over not being able to believe that it looked like such a small spot, when the church feels so big inside.

The men did what men do and sat around their table talking of fields, corn and beans. The ladies retreated to the gazebo and enjoyed their time together talking about old movies, grandchildren and a good sale.

As the conversation continued, I just took a moment and breathed in a deep gulp of air, and thanked God—a God so big, so great, so mighty—who would hear the prayers of people who didn't even know one another, yet knew the same God.

There I was, a woman praying that God would provide a headquarters, while men and women prayed that God would continue to use the church for ministry.

The great Creator truly connected the dots, connected the prayers, and connected the hearts of friends.

The journey continues.
It is unbelievably moving and emotional.
And as my friends left, one by one,
I looked up into the heavens and said to God,

*"From generation to generation
… may Your glory by known."*

❧ Good Friends & Prayer Partners ☙

LuVerne & Mona Bangsund, JaVonne Frentzel,
Walter & Mona Young, LuElla & Donald Young,
Marie & Dennis Johnson, Dean Weckwerth

The Move

*For it is God who works in you
to will and to act in order to fulfill His good purpose.*
Philippians 2:13

It was a cool lovely Monday afternoon as we stood at the church site. Our movers, Thein Moving Company, told us our prayer requests for the next day.

We needed to pray for:
- ✓ cool weather, because without that we would not be able to have the neighborhood's power turned off.
- ✓ no rain on moving day and no rain on the day before as that would create mud.
- ✓ all of the electric power companies to move quickly.

Check ... check ... check. I made mental notes and began to whisper my prayers to the God of details and order. The rains had fallen hard the day before, and although my husband, the farmer was elated for his fields of corn and soybeans, I was very nervous.

Monday had brought bright sun and a cool breeze to dry the rains, and as we stood one more time looking at the church and its home, I began to prepare mentally for the next day. We would have many media crews following us, so I wanted to walk through what I would say that would honor God and the original members and pastors of Frank Lake Church.

My hand brushed over the big old stone that had stood for 112 years to hold up the building, now sitting silent, and I looked up in the sky at the three beautiful sparrows that circled the setting. "Thank you, God," I prayed. "Thank you to each and every person who lifted these stones out of the neighboring fields and used them to stack on top of one another to create the very foundations."

Tomorrow would arrive and the church would be with us. I looked back over my shoulder.

Tuesday morning we awoke to bright sun and cool breezes. God had answered our prayers. My Best Life Ministries team arrived at the farm giggling and energized, ready to watch the monumental event.

We headed to the church site in our ministry van.

As we arrived, I heard Jason Davis telling the crowd, "Look at this, people, because you'll never see anything like it again in your lifetime." I was sure he was correct.

The television crews, newspaper staff, friends of Frank Lake Covenant, Best Life team, family, and moving crew held hands with me in a big circle as we set out to pray and trust God for the day's events.

I prayed over each person involved and asked God to protect and go before us. I shouted, "And everyone said."

The crowd answered with a joyful, "Amen!"

I shouted, "Now, let's move a church!" Cheers from the crowd were heard as we jumped in the van to lead the way.

❧ Kathleen Sogge & Kathy ❧
Ready to Lead the Way

There were several moments during the move that will be etched in my memory for my lifetime.

1. When Frank Lake Covenant Church came around the very first corner of the journey, just down the hill from its original location, Dean and I stood hand-in-hand across the soybean field and watched it from afar. It was overwhelming to hear the trucks roar, and see it moving off of its former home. But as I looked at the church side-by-side with the sweet lake it was named after, I began to cry. It would never be with its friend, the lake, again. They would no longer be together … and we watched the church move on.

2. We traveled down County Road 33 and turned to join a group of about fifty people waiting and watching from Bethesda Lutheran Church. There they sat, these wonderful people, waiting to cheer us on. They had steaming hot cups of coffee, fresh sugared donuts, chocolate chip cookies and lots of excitement!

The generations standing outside the church watching us go by spanned from little children of three years old, to several people in their eighties. A kind grandpa who was in his eighties said to me, "I'm so proud of you, young lady! Just think, they'll have her moved to your spot this afternoon, you can have church there tonight!" I laughed. He was wonderful as I watched him stand on his old blue ladder and watch for the church to come by.

As the church turned the corner and nestled in on the road next to Bethesda Lutheran, I began to cry. Side-by-side these two churches stood as the Lutheran Church rang its bells out to say a fond farewell. The little children yelled a prayer, "God bless this little church, Amen." And I thought about the stories I had heard, how these two churches had shared choirs and music from the early 1900s until the 1960s. The two friends had done great work together, and now the one waved goodbye as it sounded its forlorn bells, aching from ringing goodbye.

Bethesda Bells
Ringing Farewell

Ardell Olson
Taking a Photograph

3. As the day wore on, we had served over forty lunches to work crews, family, friends and strangers. I felt an exhaustion washing over me as the camera crew continued to ask me how I was feeling. I now listened to my husband telling stories of what had happened up to this moment.

Then we saw it, coming up over our fields of corn and soybeans. It was big and beautiful and very majestic. I looked at my dear husband, Dean, and he began to weep uncontrollably. It had been a long journey for us. Months of preparation, planning, praying, and trusting, and we were right here, right now. Much had happened, but we had so much support.

We felt the continued assurance from God that we were on the right path, His path. I hugged Dean tightly and said, "It's okay to cry." And I joined him.

❧

Coming Down the Hill Across from Frank Lake

❧

❧

Dean & Kathy
Watching the Progress

೬

Traveling Country Roads

Bridge Crossing

❦ Electric Linemen Lifting Power Lines ❧
Media Following Behind

❦

Steeple Following
the Church

❧

❧ Almost Home ☙
Traveling MN Highway 29

Our friends stood in a huddle and we sang worship songs like "How Great is Our God" and "How Great Thou Art." But when the church arrived, we sang "Amazing Grace" and cheered together! Mr. Davis leaned over and said, "With all of its tradition and heritage in music, isn't it wonderful that you are ushering it in with worship." He was right, we were ushering it in and welcoming it to a new home.

I looked at our sweet friends, Dennis and Marie Johnson, and was worried that they were okay. They said their goodbyes, but I was sure this would be an adjustment, as each person would deal with change in their own way. They have been so kind, so supportive, and I couldn't have imagined Dean and I doing this without them.

&

Prayers
&
Hymns
Welcome the
Church to the
Grove

&

Someone said to Uncle Gary, "How'd they rope you into this?" He laughed and smiled and said, "Well, I volunteered!" He stood next to Dean's folks and Gary's wife, Mary, and I felt so glad that they were with us.

My two daughters were there, and I only wished that Chandra (my middle daughter) could be there from Kansas, but she had finals. She called to say she was with us in spirit and prayers. Chandra is the impetus of the ministry, because it was the attack on her that started this journey.

My team rushed about and served people and chatted with strangers. I felt so proud of them. I looked at who each one had become, and was so happy for them.

It took about seven hours to get the church across all those miles. We heard about the delay over the railroad tracks, the slight stall out at the bridge and the close call with various power lines. Dean and I felt elated every second of the journey. Friends and neighbors hugged us and welcomed the church to the neighborhood.

Across the road stood a few timid souls, waiting at the Cashel Township Hall (old schoolhouse), watching the church coming down the road. We shouted a welcome to them, but they were comfortable watching from a distance.

Because you don't move a church every day, Dean and I wanted it to be special. We lined up two big tables and covered them with red and white checked table cloths. Then, we put out a big spread of cookies, chips, coffee and iced cold water bottles.

People milled about in excitement as Dean and I stood next to our children and Jason Davis. Davis talked about the years he'd worked for the Twin Cities news station covering miscellaneous stories, but how this story in particular was so fascinating to him. He told us he was so happy we could rescue the little church.

I remember Matt Thein saying about the move that day:

> It was nice and unusual. It's not often that we are greeted with a group of people and a band. The church move was a neat opportunity in that respect because it brought a lot of people out and drew a lot of attention, so there was quite a welcoming when it arrived at its new home. We are a recycling industry, we see the most of the buildings that would end up in a land fill and put them to use. It's gratifying to us to move it.

> My favorite part of the church move was the day it got moved and delivered to the new site. Just to see the joy on Dean and Kathy's face and the excitement about their new building arriving on their property. It's a good feeling for us to see somebody that's so happy about the project they've worked so hard to see through completion. That was truly gratifying.

When things were settled and the church was sitting on its foundation, the crowd began to dwindle. Dean and I said our goodbyes to people and walked silently hand-in-hand to see the church.

Overwhelmed and full of fatigue, I looked up at the roof of the church and said, "It's hard to believe it's finally here, here in the grove." Dean was already making plans for this and that, what needs to go here, what needs to be repaired. God's words rang out from the original scripture He gave to me as I began to pray and seek Him.

"Your people will be known as restorers of broken walls ..."

Several of our friends and family came over and joined us as we made a large circle to welcome, bless and thank God for the safe arrival of the building.

Once the church was delivered, it was set upon big blocks. We had to wait for the crew to lower it down onto its foundation. It would be a couple of weeks before that would happen.

I am sure for as long as we live; there will never be another day that equals experiencing the spiritually potent synergy that ran through the moving crew, my staff, our friends and family, and the crowd. It was truly a God-power-packed day.

But when everything was finally quiet, and the little church sat in our grove, we were ready. We were ready to get moving, but once more we had to be patient and wait for the church to be lowered down so that we could get in without a huge ladder.

As I walked in the grove one day, during my wait, I heard within its walls and windows a gentle calling to my spirit, "Awake Kathy Weckwerth, awaken Benson, awaken rural America! It's time to rise and serve."

Frank Lake Covenant had served God and people well for so many years.

It had a 32-year rest until God awakened it once again.

It was made ready to serve God once again.

Welcome home, Frank Lake Covenant Church, my new friend.

Welcome Home!

☙ We Have Lift Off! ❧

❧ Kathy & Dean Shed Tears of Joy ❦

❧ Kathy's Daughter Contemplates the Move ❦

❧ The Steeple is Removed ❧

The Steeple

Great is the Lord and most worthy of praise; His greatness no one can fathom.
One generation commends Your works to another; they tell of Your mighty acts.
Psalm 145:3

When I was a little girl growing up in southwest Iowa, I distinctly remember sitting on a little metal chair in my Sunday school class, frequently reciting the little poem with finger actions, "Here is the church, here is the steeple, open the doors and see all the people."

I fondly remember it as though it was yesterday, recalling the warm autumn sunshine that would burst through stained glass windows of the little Baptist church. Today that memory comes fully loaded to the front of my brain, ready to make me smile, remember that funny little rhyme, and put my index fingers together ... *here is the steeple!*

Journal September 17, 2012:

It has been a month since the excitement of the move of Frank Lake Covenant Church to our grove. Friends, neighbors, and media crews, all gathered as we watched the delivery of the church, and I relive it in my mind over and over, never getting sick of the replay. But today, it is quiet, and I stand alone to look over what has happened in such a short while.

The sunrays are beaming down this afternoon on the old church steeple, while I stand and watch the silver birch poplars wave lovely branches of welcome. The church building is finally reunited with its prominent architectural piece ... the steeple.

The church has been firmly attached to its new foundation, something that took only a few moments, yet distinctly made it one foot closer to getting us up into the building. Not only was the foundation secured, but I watched as the crane steadily lifted the steeple from the ground to deliver it once more to its rightful home on top of the roof.

Last Thursday, I sat on the edge of the huge moving truck and looked up, almost breathless, as Matt Thein and crew worked quickly and confidently, making sure the steeple would rest in its original spot.

As I watched, something so wonderful happened ... I saw the underside of the steeple. I had never even considered such a thing, let alone believed it would be beautiful. You see, all I've been impatiently waiting for, is a way to get into the church, counting the days, scratching them off with a big, black, magic marker ... waiting!

But somehow today, on this beautiful crisp fall morning, I sat amongst the soybeans and questioned out loud, "How is it that the things of yesterday were built with such precision, such careful expertise, such beauty?"

The underbelly of this big tin structure was overwhelmingly glorious, and as it crossed over my head, I took a deep breath in awe of the craftsmanship. Carpenters from the 1900s were suddenly at the top of my hero list for the day, as I saw a crisscross of boards all fanning together, so intricately designed. I loved the moments I could spend observing it. After all, it isn't everyday you get to see the underside of an old church steeple.

There were a few moments intermingled in the morning, where I pleasantly made my excuses to go fetch a platter of homemade sugar cookies, white sugar tops glistening in the sun, and a pitcher of fresh brewed ice tea. I had only escaped my fretting over the men on the roof and my fear for their safety for a short time.

By the time I arrived back, everything was settled, and I released a heavy sigh as Dean crossed the yard to see the day's accomplishments. I ran to meet him, breathlessly rambling on and on as I shared my thoughts of the underside of the steeple.

That was several days ago, and since then, Dean made a safe pathway to help me enter the church building on my own. Today I would enter alone. Today I would go in and look about the sanctuary in the stillness of the afternoon, and I would quiet my heart and listen.

I chose the piano bench to perch myself upon, and I pressed my fingers gently into the ivory keys playing "Faith of Our Fathers," an old hymn that I believed would honor those who devoted their service to God and this church.

Time had ticked by as I sat in the pew now, knowing it was time to walk home. But a peace, so strong, so pervading, always beckons my soul as I sat there, and I wonder about the life of the building as I pretend it shares a feeling of gladness to be resting at the farm ... in the grove.

We have found old doors from the early 1900s to replace the well-worn front doors. I look forward to their arrival, as I gently pull the old doors shut and step down the path.

Just as I am exiting, a black swallow butterfly flits by my head. He is leaving the church with me, as he has been perched on the sanctuary door. He is floating above my head towards the steeple now, and I look up and see the stature and majesty of the fixture that sets this church apart from others in its generation. The steeple ... it is plain and strong, and denotes an essence of simplistic stature.

*Here is the church ... here is the steeple ...
soon we'll be ready for the people!*

☙ Steeple is Reattached ❧

✥ The Restoration ✥

He refreshes my soul.
He guides me along the right paths
for His name's sake.
Psalm 23:3

My oldest daughter has driven past the original farm site next to her home in the Twin Cities and often commented about how lovely it was. The huge old home featured a charming wraparound porch, gables, gingerbread, and massive trees that shaded the property. Acres upon acres were given up over the years, but the original home and its trees have remained. That is … until now.

As much as society is realizing the need to reuse, redo and repurpose, the mentality that continues to supersede those ideals is progress. Whenever progress can swoop in and take one lone beautiful property and replace it with twelve single family dwellings it does—simply to fill the pockets of one human being, restoration cast to the wayside.

✥

The Church on its New Foundation

✥

The word *restoration* means, *"The action of returning something to a former owner, place, or condition."* That's what the little church needed and, unlike the lovely old home that was torn down to make way for progress, restoration would take place for the Frank Lake Covenant Church.

Our desire was to restore the church to its original condition, with a few much-needed improvements. I feel comforted and blessed to be married to someone who has learned to love old things as much as I do and has a deep respect for history.

Only a few smaller trees needed to be trimmed and there were no selfish motivations in moving the little building ... only hearts' desires that others would grow in the knowledge of Christ.

Once the church was completely settled and situated, we took a few moments to breathe before HGTV and PBS came back to interview us.

We planned out what money we had to invest in the building, worked on raising some funds for the ministry, and prioritized a list of the pertinent changes that were needed.

Dean and his brother, Gary, worked on a walkway and steps were framed and concrete was poured for the church.

❧ Dean and His Brother Gary at Work ☙

We knew that the first thing on the list was to secure the outside of the building to prevent more birds, mice, and bats from entering.

Looking for a carpenter, we found one attending our local church. He was hired to replace old rotted boards and shingles, repair the roof where the steeple had allowed water to seep in, and close up the belfry so bats could no longer reside there.

The old front doors were worn with evidence that vandals had previously tried to break and enter. We purchased two sturdy doors at an antique store for $50 to replace the old ones.

Dean began to investigate the handiwork of one of the pastors who had remodeled in the 1970s. When Dean pulled off the paneling, we found the original lovely woodwork underneath the main sanctuary doors and beautiful old beadboard that was hidden in the entry way.

With some good cleaning supplies, fresh paint in the entryway and on the siding, things on both the inside and outside were beginning to take shape.

≈ Exterior Facelift ≈

We were ready for the next major project ... the bathroom ... but we were out of funds. With all of the repairs needed to secure the outside and the rotted spots, we couldn't afford to continue to hire the carpenter.

I remember the afternoon I walked into the church. It was a dark, cold, fall afternoon. I felt dismal and remembered the night before when my husband wrote the huge check to the carpenter. That man seemed so surprised when we said we couldn't afford any more work at this time. When he left, my husband cried. The pressures, the expectations, the bank account ... it was all too much.

That afternoon I sat down on the front pew in the same spot that Mary Anderstrom had sat and prayed. I remembered her encouragement and her faith. I began to cry.

Once I finished my crying, I began to pray, just as she would. I reminded myself of His faithfulness and I reminded myself that I believed He was in this with us. I didn't have to remind myself that we were out of money. He knew and I prayed that He would provide the answer. I finished my prayer, put my jacket on, and walked home.

The next morning I received a call from my friend, JaVonne. She simply stated that she was sure we must need help and that her son and his friends from Kerkhoven, Minnesota, had a group that went out and helped others. They wanted to come over and add on a bathroom. They would do all the work if we could just help pay for the supplies.

145

The men from the Bethel Baptist Church and the Evangelical Free Church in Kerkhoven came over and worked long hours to produce a lovely, up-to-date bathroom.

The goal was to be finished by December 24 for our Christmas Eve service.

Each day ticked by and each day produced more results, but it was getting closer to our deadline. The electricity, water, and sewer had all been installed; it was just to have everything hooked up as well as getting the sink and toilet installed.

Dean stayed up half the night finishing things up and on December 24, the men were still working at the church. I paced and prayed.

At 4 p.m., the men packed up and left. The 5 p.m. service was getting ready to begin.

At 4:40 p.m. the first guest walked through the door. An eight-year-old girl, bundled up to the chin with scarf and wool coat, looked at me and said, "Do you have a bathroom?"

I happily smiled and said, "Of course, this way."

In the new year, we worked on getting the kitchen set up with a 1900's sink, also found on Craigslist, from an old house in the Twin Cities.

Bible study friends provided monies for the refrigerator and other supplies needed in the kitchen.

As we continued to host weekly Bible studies and monthly meetings, we used the church's old 1970's furnaces. Each time we started them up, a pop, shriek, and bump would come out from behind the metal slats. One day when we couldn't get the furnaces started, we hired someone to come out and look at them. He worked to get them going, only for them to shoot out sparks and start burning his eyebrows. We knew that our next priority would be to get a new cost-efficient, safe-working furnace!

❧ Removing Furnace Ductwork ☙

Throughout the past five years, due to some very generous donations to our ministry, we painted the exterior of the church, insulated the church walls, installed a new furnace and air conditioning, designed a prayer garden, restored the stained glass windows, repaired the broken circular window at the top of the south side of the church building, and created a nice parking lot.

❧ Dean Happy with Progress ❦

One of our favorite additions to the church was the original sign that sat out in front of Frank Lake Evangelical Mission Church also known as Frank Lake Covenant. Although all of the later pictures didn't show the sign, we knew that it had, at an earlier point, resided in the front yard of the church.

Dennis Johnson told us we could have anything that belonged to the church building. Dean and I dug through an old shed on the original property on a lovely sunny afternoon.

The church setting, of course, was solemn with just the cemetery remaining. A few little birds showed up to welcome us and a small bat circled around us shrieking his dismay that we were upsetting his new residence.

We dug and found a couple of missing window frames. Stowed away in the back Dean found the old sign. Dean refurbished the sign, rescued from the heaping pile, and added the name: *Best Life Ministries ~ help, hope, healing.*

I believe that the reason that I love refurbishing, rebuilding, repairing and restoration is simply because that's the relationship between God and man.

God never gives up on us and continually works to take the old broken down pieces of our lives and repurpose them.

After all, I look at my own life and that of my daughter, Chandra's. What the enemy meant for evil, God repurposed, refreshed, rejuvenated, and restored for good.

We want to continue to be like God. We want to proclaim that He provides restoration. All things worn out and broken are really, if you look close enough and dare to do a little work, restored anew through Him.

Let Him refresh your soul
and guide you along the right paths.

❧ Original Sign ❦

❧ Original Sign Refurbished ❦

The Visitors

*Do not forget to show hospitality to strangers,
for by so doing some people have shown hospitality to angels without knowing it.*
Hebrews 13:2

My first recollection of a little country-type church was a memory from age four. My parents took us to a church in the Twin Cities that was a suburb on the outskirts of the cities. The church was painted blue and sat up on a hill, far from anything else.

Every Sunday we attended, there was a little old grandpa who came to greet me. Because my own grandfather was not a personable man, this grandpa filled a need. Each Sunday, I would present him with a bird's feather I found in my yard, and each Sunday he would put it in his old fedora, smile, hug me and tell me what a nice girl I was. I believed him.

On one not so particular Sunday afternoon, he showed up at our home with a little tiny package. As children, we lived at the very end of a dead-end street. We had very little company, so when visitors arrived, we were ecstatic.

On that day, the grandpa was wearing his fedora, sporting the fresh feather I had given him a few days earlier. He handed me the package. Inside were two little bluebird lapel pins. I had never seen anything so lovely. My mother and father welcomed him in and served him coffee and cookies.

When he left, my mother said how lovely it was to have visitors. I remembered how she carefully set the table for the little lunch we would share together with our guest. The special Desert Rose Franciscan dishes came out, along with the lovely daffodil spoons, and green glasses that my siblings and I used on special occasions. While we chatted, Mom had quickly gathered a few little flowers from the yard and put them in a vase. Everything was perfect for our special visitor.

Throughout my lifetime, my parents made every visitor feel welcomed and special, whether it was for a few minutes or for a few days' stay. My daddy always said, "Kathleen, we treat people with the utmost respect, whether friends or strangers. We show them love because scripture teaches that we never know whether or not the stranger is someone in need of God's love or an angel unaware."

Somehow in time, their attitude about hospitality washed over me and stuck. I treasure the visits from strangers that I receive at the little church.

From the moment that people could walk through the doors of the church here at the grove in 2012, up until the most recent weeks, five years later, we have welcomed strangers, and served them up a generous portion of hospitality, continually using the original Frank Lake cups and plates, and adding in pretty vintage dishes and cake platters.

Elderly Couple with Bible:

One of my fondest memories was when an elderly couple drove up to the church while I was working outside. We barely had the church there a month or two. The wife got out of her car with the biggest Bible I'd ever seen and said, "We don't know what to do with this. No one in our family wants our family Bible. I know your church is Swedish and this is Norwegian, but would you keep it here for us? Could you use it?"

I smiled and thanked them. That old Norwegian Bible rests on our communion table. It resides there with us knowing that we're preserving the past within the old walls.

Luverne Sands Family:

One day in the summer of 2014, I was outside washing my car with my daughter, Jenessa. I went in the house for a few minutes when Jenessa ran in breathlessly saying, "Mom! There are several vehicles at the church and about fourteen people just walked right in!"

I thought how strange that was since I had been there the night before and distinctly remember locking the doors.

As I walked across the well-worn path to the little church, I heard loud laughing and chatter.

When I got into the church, the people continued to ignore me as I said loudly, "Hello? Hello?"

After a minute or so, a short, kind grandpa stepped out of the crowd and said, "Oh, pardon us! My name is Luverne Sands. I'm eighty-seven years old and my mommy and daddy were married here. Every time we come back to the area, my family and I drive out to the old church to visit, but this year we drove out and there was no church! We found out that it had been moved here, so we came to visit!"

The adults and children began to share how thankful they were that we saved the church, how great it looked, how peaceful the setting was, and how their family had several Covenant pastors that had served or were still serving in churches.

Mostly that day, I was drawn to Luverne. I offered the family cookies *(which I learned to keep stockpiled in the freezer)* and as they munched on them, I learned about their family and they learned about ours.

When the Sands family headed out the front doors, I told Luverne and his wife about how surprised I was that they could get in the church since I had pulled the door and made sure it was locked the night before.

I'll never forget what he said in response! "You may think that you locked the door, but God unlocked it for us today. You'll never know how much this meant to us. What you're doing is such good work for God. You were meant for this little church and it was meant for you. Keep up the good work." Then, he and his wife hugged me tightly and he whispered in my ear, "I'm so proud of you." It was just as if my own daddy, who has been passed for seven years, was there whispering in my ear.

Unknown Family:

On another warm sunny day, a woman called to see if her family could stop by and visit the church. The woman looked me squarely in the eye and said, "Thank you! Thank you for carrying on the work for those people who built this building, and served all those years. You are continuing a piece of their history. You are continuing their worship."

I never did get her name.

Friends from Bethel Baptist Church:

One lovely September evening, friends of mine from a Kerkhoven church came over to visit. I proudly walked them through the building, sharing the deep, rich history. I showed them photos, pews, the piano, and served them coffee from the old church coffee cups that Marie Johnson so kindly gave to me when they sold me the church.

As the ladies sat down for coffee and we shared bites of sugary cookies, one woman looked up to an old photo on the wall and said, "Look! There's Grandpa!"

I was surprised when another woman said, "Yes, I was married here." And then one by one, they told of how they grew up in the church, were married there, and how family members attended confirmation classes and services right at our church.

Mrs. Wilhamine Huber:

On a lovely fall day in 2012, Dean brought home a small brown envelope for me from a dear old lady. Inside was a picture of the church from 1917. She wrote this to me in her letter:

> *I decided to write to you and thank you for saving a beautiful old church! Frank Lake Covenant Church has special meaning to me because long ago it was my grandparents' home-church and where my mother went to Sunday school and was confirmed. My mother's name was Winnie Hallberg and her family farmed in Swift County until 1917, when they moved to New London. I remember going with my parents to visit her old friends and attending Frank Lake a few times.*

She said her deepest desire was to have her daughter bring her out to see the building one last time.

Dr. Richard Carlson and Dr. Kent Molde

In mid-July of 2016, I experienced one of my all-time favorite visitors. Reverend Nils Frykman's great-grandson, Dr. Richard Carlson, visited with his long-time friend, Dr. Kent Molde.

Journal Entry, Wednesday, July 13, 2016:

The rumble of a farm truck driving by snapped me out of my quiet contemplations and I looked down at my phone to see an email. Dr. Kent Molde, formerly from the area, asked me if he could bring his friend, Dr. Richard Carlson, to see the church. His friend was related to one of the church's former pastors.

Whenever the past and present intermingle, Dean and I anxiously anticipate how God will reveal a story. I hurried home to stir up some of Grandma Thelma's sugar cookies for the visit. We would be entertaining the great-grandson of my beloved Rev. Nils Frykman.

I looked up as three gleeful robins danced and flapped their wings amidst the bubbling water of the fountain. A lovely white butterfly circled above my head, being blown to and fro in the gentle breeze, and I believed that even nature was celebrating with me over this joyous occasion. We would meet a living descendant from the pastor I had studied so diligently ... the pastor I loved.

The next morning arrived with bright sunshine and the air had a reverent stillness that settled above the building. Dean and I happily greeted the visitors and learned of their longtime friendship. Kent had sent Richard a link to watch our church move when Richard realized that it was the same church his great-grandpa had served.

While the men walked into the building, I watched Richard's face as he soaked in the air of days gone by and settled his focus on the wall where Nils' pictures hung.

Richard stated, "This is a remarkable experience ... a time warp. I feel very emotional. To look at the pulpit where my great-grandfather spoke is a remarkable thing. I heard a lot about this church, but never saw it."

Richard stood by Nils' portrait, painted by Swift County artist and former Frank Lake Covenant member Mamie Falk, and we caught our breath. The resemblance was extraordinary, as though the paintbrush of time had gently stroked through the years of DNA and washed across the Creator's canvas to craft the man who now stood before us.

I wondered what it would have been like to have the genetics of this incredible preacher songwriter running through my veins. Did it sink in that this relative made such an impact on others? Richard shared, "Yes, he did have a huge impact. Growing up in the Covenant church we would sing his hymns and talk about him. He was a revered figure in the history of the evangelical church, so we feel very proud to be part of his ancestry."

Our time together ended and I felt sadness as the doctors left. For a brief moment in time, everything in our little world had come full circle. The revered pastor had been talked about, honored, and we felt close to him ... closer than ever.

Later, I received a note from Richard stating words that brought a soothing balm over past hurts, a resonating tenacity over the daily journey and an encouraging hope for tomorrow.

> *Dear Kathy and Dean,*
>
> *I was truly moved by the opportunity to visit the relocated Frank Lake Church, to view the Nils Frykman photos, and to experience actually standing behind the pulpit from which my great-grandfather preached on so many occasions.*
>
> *You have done such a wonderful thing in lovingly restoring this historic worship building.*
>
> *On behalf of the entire extended Frykman family I can say how much we appreciate that this church, which has a very special meaning in our family life, has been both lovingly restored and also returned to its purpose of serving the Lord.*
>
> *With Love and Appreciation, Richard Carlson*

James 'Jim' Roe:

Another favorite visit was from a man named Jim Roe. Jim was an eighty-year-old woodworker when he came to visit the church to see if he could restore our pulpit. Every time I tried to stand and speak behind it, I was overshadowed by its enormous size.

When Dean turned it over on its side, he discovered it too had been covered with 1970's paneling. Jim would try to refurbish what had once been the pastor's pulpit that dated all the way back to 1900.

When Jim returned the pulpit, we were amazed at his craftsmanship. He had taken a few pieces from other remnants of old churches and used them to complete the cut-up podium. We were very grateful for the art of renovation and restoration, of preserving and embracing history.

❧ Jim Roe ☙
Delivering Restored Pulpit

Marlene Hauge:

One May afternoon, Best Life Ministries was hosting its annual women's one-day event at the little church. My friend and great encourager for the history of Frank Lake Covenant, Marlene Carlson Hauge, from Kerkhoven arrived at the event. Marlene is happy to have the church still being used.

During our lunch time, I heard her telling others, "This is where we had our Sunday school classes," as she pointed to Frank Lake's side room. And as she looked to the front of the church, she remarked with a smile, "This is where I said I do!"

⁂ Marlene Carlson Hauge Wedding ⁂
December 12, 1964

❧ Christmas 2013 ❦

Truck Driver:

One dark cold December day in 2015, I opened the mail to find a check with a short note attached. It was from a truck driver who drove Highway 29 frequently.

He wrote that one night in early December he was feeling so lost and discouraged. As he approached the church that night, he remembered attending church as a little boy and was drawn to the warm lights that were shining out from the sanctuary across the snowy fields.

The note continued by explaining that in those fleeting moments of driving by, he felt like God called to him, *"Come back to me."* He wanted me to know what had happened and wanted to support our work.

Donna Mae Mikkelson:

One lovely spring afternoon, I had a woman from our town call and ask if she could bring her mother out to celebrate her ninetieth birthday. She said her mother had attended the church as a little child.

When the ninety-year-old walked through the church doors, she exclaimed, "Oh, I remember this. It's all coming back to me."

We spent the afternoon together with a little lunch of homemade cookies and *rømmegrøt* (a decadent cream porridge or pudding) that they brought to celebrate the birthday.

I gave a short devotion and we sang hymns together. When we got to the hymn, *"Children of the Heavenly Father,"* I sang the first verse in Swedish, just as I did for Dennis Johnson the first day I arrived at the church.

I looked up to see the dear woman and her daughter wiping tears from their eyes.

Nancy Gustafson:

On a cold March afternoon in 2013, I received a lovely note from Nancy. I was surprised when I opened the envelope and saw a beautiful watercolor of Frank Lake Covenant. She told me that Fern Nelson, who attended her church, First Covenant, Willmar, Minnesota, had a lawyer-son who lived out west and loved to paint rural churches. I am thankful that she found the painting and sent it to me.

Denny Thompson:

On July 20, 2015, I received an email from Denny Thompson thanking me for moving the church. He lived in Faribault, Minnesota. He explained to me that his grandmother, Freda Dahl, had been the church's organist in the early 1900s. His great-grandparents had attended Frank Lake Covenant. He, his daughter and grandson, along with his cousin and wife from the state of Washington wanted to come out to the little church for a visit on August 5, 2015.

Journal Entry August 8, 2015:

Whenever I have an extra moment in time, I research our little church. I look for pictures, newspaper clippings, and people who still remember what took place so long ago. At times, I am blessed with a surprise photo or ... a visitor.

Not long ago, I received a message from a kind man named Denny Thompson, requesting that he and his family might come to visit us at the church where his family attended from 1904-1924.

I prepared the church by sweeping, dusting, and baking up fresh cookies for the occasion.

The morning the Thompsons arrived was warm and sunlight filled the church building casting rainbows of light on the floors and church pews. When they stepped out of their car, I felt an immediate kinship; after all, they were relatives of people who attended this very same building back in the early 1900s, the same building I use each and every day.

As we discussed the church, the family, and the history, they sang one of the hymns that Reverend Nils Frykman wrote and we enjoyed a hymn-sing at the piano.

I had been struggling earlier that week with an onslaught of self doubt. Not the kind that creeps in every once and awhile when you're tired, no this was deeper and was seeping in through cracks and crevices in my confidence level. I wondered if I was doing anything that mattered. Working each day writing, speaking, praying, teaching, leading, singing, and now adding in a weekly radio show, I just wondered if I was making any difference in this world.

And then it happened, as I listened to Denny tell the story of his family the Dahls and their connection to our little church, I felt a kinship connection once again and allowed my mind to travel back with theirs in time.

I listened as Denny talked about his great-grandparents and their arrival to the Murdock area in the early 1900s and how they attended the church. His grandmother, Alfreda 'Freda' Dahl, was church organist. I looked at the picture of her fine features and soft eyes and could imagine her up front accompanying the congregation.

Denny explained that his great-grandparents Charles and Christina, their seven children, and his mother, Marion, all attended the little church Denny explained that two of the relatives had become pastors.

But then he did something strange as I told about my own journey that led us to buy the church. In a very gentle manner, much like my late daddy would act, he looked straight at me and said, "Thank you, Kathy, for all you're doing to carry on the legacy of this church. Thank you." I bit my lip to try to stop crying, but tears did trickle down my cheek.

Denny gave me old photographs and copies of his great-aunt Esther's journal. As I perused the pages of history, it was as if I was standing on their front lawn, outside of Murdock, observing the family's everyday life.

As owner of the little church, I was encouraged as I read about the community of neighbors. They went to church Sundays and Wednesdays, ate together after meetings, participated in various clubs that supported the church and loved and served God.

Throughout the storms, the dust, and the bitter blizzard days, they made their way to the little building and worshipped together, and it made them stronger. The core of their being was striving to be their best amidst adverse challenges. And in the journal that I read from 1910, there were no questions as to whether or not they mattered, or for that fact anything mattered.

For me, on days when I question or doubt, I remember the kind words of Denny, whose family walked before me.

I remember the words he said.

> "Thank you for carrying on the legacy of my family
>
> and those who went before us ... their purpose,
>
> their faith lives on in you and your work."

~ Summer 2015 ~

The Journey Continues

Know therefore that the Lord your God is God,
the faithful God who keeps covenant and steadfast love with those who love Him
and keep His commandments, to a thousand generations.
Deuteronomy 7:9

There are times in one's life when monumental moments are created. Dreams become realities, and we look over our shoulder at what once was and what has become.

The move was a story that we would not experience again, and one that had a great impact on many lives.

Frank Lake Church was settled into the grove and its name was changed to Church in the Grove, but its heart, its memories, and its congregants who created the dream and followed through with it as far as it would go on the road they traveled, would always be kept alive as long as Dean and I own it.

The fall of 2012 was lovely and brought exciting new opportunities. For those who questioned why we would move a church and what we were going to do with it, Dean and I prayed and sought God for direction on what we should do at the church.

I knew that I wanted to begin women's Bible studies. With that plan in place, I invited several of the neighbors and friends to come once a week to study God's Word together.

The more that I sought a women's study that would be Christ-centered, an easy format and good for various denominations, the more I realized that I couldn't find anything appropriate for our needs. I set out to create my own Bible studies and wrote three ten-week studies that we use and that I offer for sale at our Best Life Ministries conferences and on my website.

Along with the Bible studies, we hold Christmas Eve services, monthly services, wedding and baby showers, weddings, baptisms, and host various women's gatherings.

My favorite days, of course, were the days when visitors connected to our little church would just show up unannounced, and soak in the history of yesteryears.

Many events happened and the church found a place on the 'map' of surrounding communities. We knew that when our friends called to ask if they could host their Christmas wedding on December 23, 2013, we couldn't refuse.

That evening, the pastor who would officiate showed up early. He was a young man who was very happy and kind. Grandma Thelma would have described him as a man "generous of heart."

He walked into the church and took his time looking at each and every photo, studying each face and each description, and asking several pertinent questions about the history of the church.

We busied ourselves as we prepared for the wedding and everything went smoothly. No one knew that four hours beforehand, Dean had been desperately trying to get the old furnaces up and running. For whatever reason, the only time they seemed to work was when we prayed over them, and then they'd fire right up!

I remember that night and how I thought about all of the weddings that had taken place over the history of the church. I had at least four pictures of wedding couples ranging from 1913-1966.

I thought about the description of Mamie Anderson's wedding to August Falk on December 7, 1917 at 7:00 p.m. at the little church. The description I read from the *Raymond News*, the Raymond, Minnesota, newspaper was lovely.

> *Little Viola Strandberg, daintily dressed in pink satin messaline, was the flower girl and Ardel Berg was ring bearer, carrying the ring in the heart of a rose.*
>
> *The bride was attended by the Misses Hilma and Alice Falk, sisters of the groom, who were gowned in pink satin messaline with an over drape of silk net. They carried arm bouquets of pink carnations. The bride's gown was of ivory satin fashioned with a train and an over drape of Georgette crepe and was trimmed with a garniture of pearls.*
>
> *The veil was held in place by a wreath of smilax, she carried a shower bouquet of bride's roses.*
>
> *The church was decorated with pink and white streamers and green foliage and the lights were shaded to soften the color schemes.*

The first wedding at our grove was a little more simplistic. That night had neither bridesmaids nor groomsmen, nor flower girls and pink carnations. Instead, it was plain and simple with the bride wearing a beautiful knee-length white lace dress and the groom wearing a black shirt and pants with a white tie.

When the ceremony was finished, I felt a sense of satisfaction that the little church had made its way through Bible studies, church services, a pie social and now a wedding. Life in the church was back in full force, as it was being used for God's glory once again.

After the final blessing, the small crowd made its way out the doors and I was left standing with the jolly pastor. He turned to me and said, "This church hadn't finished its purpose yet, Kathy. The destiny that God set before it had not yet been accomplished. I'm so glad you and Dean picked up what had been set down, and were able to partner with God to get it moving once again. It's being used for God and that's an amazing feat. Bless you and bless the future of this little building." And then he walked out.

Since that evening, several years have passed. I keep close in my heart the pastor's words and believe each day that Dean and I are responsible to keep alive the dream and vision that C. M. Youngquist and the original congregation held.

Mamie Anderson & August Falk
December 7, 1917

History notes of the church, taken December 20, 1948, mention that during those beginning years of starting the Swedish Evangelical Mission Church of Frank Lake, Youngquist and others saw *"a real spirit of revival at that time and many souls gave their hearts to the Lord."*

There are many days that I spend at the little church. Often I go over in the early morning, brew a pot of coffee, and sit down in Grandma Mary's spot on the front pew to pray.

I frequently review the connections and heart strings that tie the little church with mine. My soul resonates specifically with four Frank Lake Covenant individuals.

1) **Reverend C. W. Youngquist**
   Charles was a visionary. He saw things far into the future, knew how to plan, and loved God with all he was.

When coming to the Twin Cities and meeting with the other Covenant pastors, Charles followed God in helping to create the vision that would lead to people in rural Murdock, Minnesota, meeting to worship. Charles followed the dream and followed God, even if it took work and didn't completely make sense. After all, why start a church in rural Minnesota? Like Charles, I say, "Why not?"

My whole life has continually been about creating a vision and leading people to that vision. Whether it was in church services or a nonprofit, I followed God, then led and people followed me.

Vision-casting and making the dream come to life has always been my passion.

2) **Reverend Nils Frykman**
   Nils had so much trouble throughout his life trying to serve God. The school in Sweden did not want him, so he left there, moved with his family to Chicago and became a pastor. The church did not want him and he was not rehired. God ended up blessing him by sending him to Pennock, Minnesota, where he would become a circuit pastor and write over 300 hymns for the Covenant association.

When I was twelve, I started writing songs and by age twenty-five, I had over fifty Christian songs that I had written and was singing for events. It was one of my happiest joys in life, to be inspired, to write and then to sing and share it with others.

As much as I'd like to convey that my twenty-eight years of serving churches went smoothly, I cannot say that. I had great difficulty and even my last church hosted a new pastor who didn't want a woman worship director. But God blessed me, and in my leaving, He helped me create a nonprofit, allowed me the privilege of purchasing a church and serving where God is my boss, and He inspired me to write five books.

3) **Reverend Sven Roslin**
   After serving in Chicago, Rev. Roslin served the Evangelical Covenant Church in Stanton and Boone, Iowa. Then, he came to work at Frank Lake Covenant and the circuit churches for about three years. Roslin was a hard worker and during his time pastoring, the inside of the sanctuary at Frank Lake was renovated and the exterior was painted.

Growing up in Iowa, one of my greatest joys as a little child was driving through Stanton, Iowa (about twenty miles from my home) to get to church in Red Oak, Iowa. As we would drive through, I would stare up at the big old Covenant church in awe. During the Christmas season, it was the most beautiful church as the stained glass windows reflected colorful hues amidst the wintry snow.

I would have never believed that some forty-six years later, I would own a church that I was helping to restore and renovate, whose pastor once served at the beautiful church in Stanton, Iowa, which I admired as a child.

4) **Esther Forsell**
According to those I interviewed, Esther loved music, loved leading the children and was so happy to be able to serve at the church using her gifts.

When I turned twelve, I began playing piano for our church service, as they had no one else available to lead the music. Thus began my lifetime career working with music. One of my first duties, during my years of working as a Director of Worship and Creative Arts, was to lead a seventy-five member children's choir. This became a part of my role in all of the churches I served and I loved watching the hearts of children as they worshiped Jesus.

To be like those souls from 1900 and carry on God's providential destiny has always been our plan since we purchased the building. That is our hearts' cry. Over and over we have prayed for God to bring revival to the rural communities of Minnesota, just as C. M. Youngquist did.

Our hearts continue to turn to God and lay our hurting world at His feet. We pray that churches will stay true to God's Word. We pray that people will turn their hearts and minds back to God. We ask God for forgiveness for where we've gone wrong and ask Him to help us find our way, just as did Reverend Nils Frykman.

We will keep working on restoring and renovating until the little church is completed and sound, just as Reverend Sven Roslin renovated.

We pray to bring healing to the hurting, to bring music and worship to the needy soul and to bring God's restoration to the people who attend our little church just as Esther Forsell.

In the words of Reverend Nils Frykman's song, "*Min framtidsdag är ljus och lång*" ("I Have a Future All Sublime"), it ends like this: "Dear Lord, I pray that I may be more wholly yielded unto thee, while on the way I yet remain, before my heav'nly home I gain."

The words of this song are the prayer of Dean and Kathy.

Today the church sits proudly, tucked amidst the large poplars and tall evergreens in the grove. For many who drive by, they believe the little church has always been there. But for Dean and Kathy Weckwerth, we know that this was certainly, for us personally and for Frank Lake Covenant Church ... *the move of a lifetime.*

❧
Church in the Grove Interior
❧

And His mercy is on them that fear Him
... from generation to generation
Luke 1:50

❧ Dean & Kathy Weckwerth ☙
On the Steps of Church in the Grove
Fall 2013

Frank Lake Covenant Church
Before the Move

Church in the Grove
After the Move

❧ Moonlit Evening 2014 ❧

♦ December 2015 ♦

☙ December 2016 ❧

INDEX

Page numbers in italics indicates photos

A
Altrogge, Mark 88
Anderson, A. J., Mrs. 54
Anderson, Alice (Magnuson) 14
Anderson, Andrew John (Andrew Johan Jonasson) 64
Anderson, Axel 6, 8
Anderson, Lizzy (Berg) 49, 64
Anderson, Rev. C. D. 26
Anderson, Fred 14
Anderson, Jonas 64
Anderson, Hattie 62
Anderson, Mamie (Falk) (Bergstrom) 49, 54, 55, 56, 64, 67, 155, 164, *165*
Anderstrom, Mary 90, 91, 92, 119, 145, 166
Anderson, Sophia 64
Anfinson, Reed 87, 105
Applegren, Michelle 59
Aspinall, Will 109

B
Bangsund, LuVerne 'Vernie' 74, 75, 119, 120, *114*
Bangsund, Mona 74, 119, 120, *114*
Bengtson, Marian 26
Bengtson, Rev. Reuben 26
Berg, Alfred 14
Berg, Ardel 164
Berg, Elizabeth 'Lizzy' Christine (Anderson) 49, 64
Berg, Emma 27
Berg, Emanual 164
Berg, Maria Christina 49
Berg, Olaus Olson 'O. O.' 6, 8, 49, 54, 64, 67
Berg, Otto 14
Berggren, J. F. 27
Bergstrom Family 49
Bergstrom, Axel Leonard 67
Bergstrom, Emma Adelia (Sands) 66, 67
Bergstrom, L. 67
Bergstrom, Mamie (Anderson) (Falk) 49, 54, 55, 56, 64, 67, 155, 164, *165*
Bergstrom, Mary 67
Bergstrom, William 'Bill' 66

Bethel Baptist Church Friends 146, 153
Bloom, Rev. Able 26
Bjork, Carl August 24, 27
Boquist, C. W. 27

C
Carlson, Aaron 24
Carlson, Anna 26, 34
Carlson, Rev. A. W. 8, 21, 26, 34, 67
Carlson, Anna (Larson) 34, 42, 60
Carlson, Clarence 62
Carlson, Dick 103, 104
Carlson, Donald 63
Carlson, Emma 50
Carlson, Eric 104
Carlson, Dr. Richard 32, *154*, 155
Carlson, Joseph 50
Carlson, Juliet 49
Carlson, Marlene (Hauge) 47, *48*, 157
Carlson, Olaf 49, 50
Carlson, Reynold 49, *62*
Challman, Hannah 26
Challman, Rev. Lars B. 26
Chryst, Emma (Dahl) 52
Clark, Walter 63

D
Dahl Family 49, 52, 160
Dahl, Adla (Franklin) 52, 53
Dahl, Anna Alfreda 'Freda' (Larson) 51, 52, 53, 160
Dahl, Augusta (Forsell) 49, *56*
Dahl, Axel 53
Dahl, Carl (Rueben) 53
Dahl, Charles (Carl) 6, 51, 52, 53, 56
Dahl, Christina 51, 52, 53, 56, 160
Dahl, Emma (Chryst) 52
Dahl, Esther 29, *51*, 53
Dahl, Mable 53
Dahl, Marvin 62
Dahl, Rueben 53
Danielson, Edwin 6, 8
Davis, Jason 87, 123, 131, 132

E
Edoff, C. J. 27
Ellson, Charles 'Snickare Charlie' 6
F
Falk, Alice 164, *165*
Falk, August 54, 164, *165*
Falk, Bonnie 59
Falk, Hilma 164, *165*
Falk, Mamie (Anderson) (Bergstrom) 49, 54, 55, 56, 64, 67, 155, 164, *165*
Falk, Richard 56
Falk, Wendall 102
Felt Family 49
Felt, Eldon 59
Felt, Evelyn 59
Felt, Nina (Johnson) 62
Forsell, Augusta (Johnson) 49, *56*
Forsell, Charles G. 49, *56*
Forsell, Charlotte *16*, 59
Forsell, Esther (Johnson) 52, 56, 57, 58, 62, 167
Forsell, Pearl 49
Forsell, Merry (Netland) *44*, *48*
Forsell, Olivia 56
Forsell, Oscar 49, 62
Fost, Mary Edelia *14*
Franklin, Adla (Dahl) 52, *53*
Franklin, Immanuel 'Benjie' 52
Frentzel, JaVonne 74, 120, *122*, 145
Frykman, Andrew 'AT' *31*, 32
Frykman, Anna *31*, 32
Frykman, Betty 26, *31*
Frykman, Carl *31*, 32
Frykman, Gust *31*, 32
Frykman, Hilma *31*, 32
Frykman, Nathanial *31*, 32
Frykman, Rev. Nils (Larrson) 8, *11*, 13, 21, 24, 26, 28, 29, 30, *31*, 32, 51, 55, 67, 68, *154*, 155, 160, 166, 167
Frykman, Oscar *31*, 32
Frykman, Otto *31*, 32
Frykman, Paul *31*, 32
Frykman, Victor *31*, 32
G
Graberg, J. F. 27
Grossman, Jenessa 71, 132, *135*, 152
Gustafson, Helen 26
Gustafson, J. 27
Gustafson, Nancy 159
Gustafson, Rev. Ervil 26
H
Hallberg Family 49
Hallberg, Anna 57
Hallberg, Emil 57
Hallberg, Winnie Violet (Johnson) 46, 57, 153
Hallner, Andrew 27
Hanson, Caren 90, 91, 92
Harstad, Frank 5
Hauge, Marlene (Carlson) 55, 56, 57, 80, 165
Herring, Dave 105
Hildebrand, Dr. Chandra 71, 132, 149
Holmberg, Janet 59
Holmberg, Jeanne 59
Hookenson, Elsie 49
Hookenson, Roy 49
Huber, Wilhamine (Johnson) 46, 57, 153
Hultman, J. A. 27
I
Iskierka, Alexis 71, 72, 132, 141
J
Johnson Family 49
Johnson, Albert 59
Johnson, Amanda 62
Johnson, Andrew 6, 8
Johnson, August 6
Johnson, Augusta (Jonasson) 64
Johnson, Charles (Carl Jonasson) 6, 8, 64
Johnson, Clarence 57
Johnson, Dennis 59, 62, 63, 80, *81*, 82, 83, 84, 92, 98, 101, 102, 104, 110, *112*, 113, 119, 120, *122*, 131, 149, 159
Johnson, Diane 59
Johnson, Dorothy 59

Johnson, Dorothy 59
Johnson, Edwin 33, 62
Johnson, Rev. Edwin S. 23, 26, *43*
Johnson, Ernest *12*, 15, 57
Johnson, Esther (Forsell) 52, 56, 57, *58*, 62, 167
Johnson, Ervin 62, *67*
Johnson, Helen 59
Johnson, K. A. 27
Johnson, Kathleen 59
Johnson, Kathy *48*
Johnson, Margaret 82
Johnson, Marie 59, 62, *81*, *84*, 98, 101, 102, 110, *112*, 119, *122*, 131, 153
Johnson, Nina (Felt) 62
Johnson, Pearl 57
Johnson, Raymond 57, 62
Johnson, Richard 59
Johnson, Ronald 59
Johnson, Viola 26
Johnson, Walfred 14
Johnson, Wilhamine (Huber) 46, 57, 153
Johnson, Winnie Violet (Hallberg) 46, 57, 153
Jonasson, Andrew Johan (Andrew John Anderson) 64
Jonasson, Carl (Charles Johnson) 6, 8, 64

L
Larson Family 64
Larson, Anna (Carlson) 34, 42, 60
Larson, Anna Alfreda 'Freda' (Dahl) *51*, 52, 53, 160
Larson, Carol 63
Larson, Claude *14*
Larson, Claus 33, *67*
Larson, Dianne *16*, 52
Larson, Ella *12*, *14*
Larson, Ellen 14
Larson, Emma 67
Larson, Ethel *12*, 67
Larson, Evelyn 62
Larson, Harry 49, 52
Larson, Howard 49
Larson, Jennifer *16*, 52
Larson, L. P. 6, 8
Larson, Marion (Thompson) 51, 52, 161
Larson, Lars Peter 64
Larson, Thure *14*, 64
Larson, Vernie (Swenson) 11, *12*, 29, 49, 67, *68*
Larson, Violet 'Vye' 49
Lindell, J. P. 27
Lindell, Mary Ellen 59
Lundgren, Marilyn 26, 42
Lundgren, Rev. Richard 26, 42, *43*, *48*, 49, 101, 104

M
Magnuson, Alice (Anderson) 14
Magnuson, Susan 59
Matson, S. A. 24
Mellander, Axel 24
Mellgren Family 49
Mellgren, John 6
Mikkelson, Donna Mae 159
Moberg, Alf 65
Moberg, Amy 65
Moberg, Esther 65
Moberg, Martin 65
Moberg, Tena 65
Molde, Dr. Kent 154
Morgan, Cindy 104

N
Neal Clarence Jr. 63
Neal, Lavilla 63
Nelson, Ardell 59
Nelson, Fern 159
Nelson, Rev. Albin E. 4, 22, 26, *39*
Nelson, Violet 26, *39*
Netland, Merry (Forsell) *44*, *48*
Norsen, Goran 27

O
Olson Family 49
Olson, Ardell 124, *125*
Olson, Gary *48*
Olson, Janice *16*, 59
Ostling, Ester 26, 35

Ostling, Rev. Arvid Jacob 'AJ' 21, 26, 35

P
Palm, Alice 62
Palm, Marie 62
Paulson, Amanda 26
Paulson, Theodore J. Rev. 25, 26
Peterson, C. G. 24
Peterson, J. 27

R
Reinertson, Rev. Martin 26, 38
Roe, James 'Jim' 156
Roslin, Christine 26, 37
Roslin, Rev. Sven Emil (Josefsson) 21, 26, 37, 62, 166, 167

S
Sahlstrom, C. O. 27
Sallman, Warner 18, 20, 80
Sands Family 49, 152
Sands, Charles Oscar 66, 67
Sands, Dewey 67
Sands, Donald 67
Sands, Dorothy 67
Sands, Emma Adelia (Bergstrom) 66, 67
Sands, Harlie 67
Sands, James 67
Sands, Luverne 67, 152
Sands, Muriel 67
Sands, Virgil 67
Sands, Winfield 67
Schultz, Rev. Lewie 104
Silver, Rob 109, 112
Skogsbergh, E. August 27
Slaathaug, Rev. Dennis 26
Slaathaug, Shirley 26
Soderstrom, J. F. 27
Sogge, Jim 119
Sogge, Kathleen 79, 80, 91, 119, *124*
Steinert, Alma 26
Steinert, Theo 8
Steinert, Rev. Theodore 21, 26, *32, 33*, 34, 68,
Stenlund, Carol 63
Stenlund, Myra 26, *40*
Stenlund, Rev. Eddie R. 23, 26, *40, 41*, 63
Strandberg, Viola 164
Sundberg, Rev. A. 6, 26, *28*
Swenson, Ethel 67
Swenson, George 67
Swenson, Vernie (Larson) 11, *12*, 29, 49, 67, *68*

T
Thein, Jim 87, 93, 109, *110*, 123
Thein, Matt 109, *110*, 111, 123, 132, 137
Thein, Tim 109, *110*, 123
Thompson, Denny 52, 160, 161
Thompson, Marion (Larson) 51, 52, 161
Turnquist Family 49
Turnquist, Laura 63

V
Vast, Frank 5

W
Wass, John 6, 9, 34
Wallbom, C. 24
Weckwerth, Bud 119, 132
Weckwerth, Dean 2, 62, 74, 75, 80, 82, 83, 84,85, 87, *89*, 91, 92, 93, 94, 95, 97,101, 109, 112, 114, *117*, 118, 119, 120, 121, 122, 124, 126, *127*, *131*, 132, 135, 138, 142, 144, 146,148, 149, 153, 154, 155, 156, 163, 164, 167, *169*
Weckwerth, Gary 132, *142*
Weckwerth, Kathy (Where Kathy is mentioned by name ~ really every page!) 62, 75, 82, 83, 86, 89, 90, 103, 111, *116*, 124, *127*, 132, 133, *135*, 151, 155, 161, 164, 167, *169*
Weckwerth, Marion 74, 119, 132
Weckwerth, Mary 132
Wedin, P. 27
Wennerberg Family 49
Wenstrand, Andrew E. 27
Wenstrand, John 24

Y
Young, Donald 74, 75, 119, 120, *122*
Young, LuElla 74, 75, 83, 119, 120, *122*,
Young, Mona 74, 119, 120, *122*

Young, Walter 119, *122*
Youngquist, Rev. C. M. (Charles Magnus) 5, *6*, 8, 26, 27, 45, 164, 166, 167
Youngquist, Emma 26
Youngquist, Sven A. 24
Youmans, Duane C. 82, 83, 151
Youmans, Leta C. 151
Youmans, Thelma L. 151, 163

Z
Zakrison, N. P. 27
Zempel, Maxine 91

About the Author

Kathy A. Weckwerth is Founder and Executive Director of the nonprofit ministry, Best Life Ministries. She is an author, blogger, motivational speaker, Bible study facilitator and radio host of YOUR BEST with Kathy Weckwerth found on iTunes, SoundCloud, and Stitcher.

Kathy and her husband, Dean, live in rural Minnesota next door to their 1900's church that serves as Best Life Ministries' headquarters.

Other books by Kathy: *Putting the Pieces Together: A Worship Director's Guide*, three 10-week Bible studies: *be.attitudes*, *Joseph: The Story of My Life*, and *Blaze Your Trail*.

www.kathyweckwerth.com

bestlifeministries.com